Curly Bill

Tombstone's Most Famous Outlaw

CURLY BILL

Illustration of Curly Bill courtesy Bob Boze Bell.

Curly Bill

Tombstone's Most Famous Outlaw

Steve Gatto

Protar

House

P.O. Box 14007
Lansing, Michigan 48901

ISBN # 0-9720910-2-5 (Hardcover)
ISBN # 0-9720910-3-3 (Softcover)

First Edition: July 2003

Protar House
P.O. Box 14007
Lansing, Michigan 48901

CONTENTS

Acknowledgments

I would like to thank the many institutions throughout the country for their continuing work in preserving a wealth of documents that enable researchers to find details about Old West characters and incidents. The collections housed in the Arizona Historical Society Library and the University of Arizona Library are valuable resources to anyone researching Curly Bill. In addition, the Arizona State Archives in Phoenix, Arizona; the New Mexico State Archives in Sante Fe, New Mexico; the University of New Mexico Library and Special Collections Department in Albuquerque, New Mexico; the Texas State Archives in Austin, Texas; and the Library of Michigan in Lansing, Michigan, provided much material for review.

No research could be done without the various county courthouses and court clerk's offices that have maintained records. Among these I would like to thank the staffs of the Cochise County Clerk's Office, Bisbee, Arizona; Pima County Clerk's Office, Tucson, Arizona; El Paso County Clerk's Office, El Paso, Texas; and the Grant County Court Clerk's Office, Silver City, New Mexico.

Over the years many individuals have aided me in researching the Old West. I would like to thank Neil Carmony, editor of John Clum's *Apache Days and Tombstone Nights* (1997), for his thoughts on the Old West. Thanks also to Dave Johnson, author of *John Ringo* (1996), who started me on the trail of Curly Bill several years ago. Additional thanks to Ben T. Traywick, Tombstone's official town historian, for his assistance over the years. The documents he has reproduced in his own books have been important sources of information. Manny Alvarez and his wife Sonia, as well have provided assistance and encouragement to me over the years. I would also like to thank Ted Liliensteins for his work on the cover illustration for this book. I am also grateful to Bob Boze Bell, editor of *True West* magazine, for allowing me to use his illustration of Curly Bill in this book.

Bob Pugh of *Trail to Yesterday Books* in Tucson, book collector "Mickey V," and Kevin Mulkins, a dedicated collector of Tombstone books and documents, deserve acknowledgment for their moral support and encouragement. Finally, a special thanks goes out to Curly Bill. Trailing his life has been a true challenge and rewarding experience for an Old West researcher.

PREFACE

My search for Curly Bill, Tombstone's most famous outlaw, began in 1993. While driving from Michigan to Arizona during a semester break from law school, I stopped in Zionsville, Indiana, to visit a friend. Like myself, Dave Johnson was researching the life of John Ringo, the Texas-Arizona cowboy, who was a legendary Western figure. I had spent the past several years tracking down information about Ringo, but did not know what I might do after completing a book on the infamous cowboy. While we were talking and looking at documents from Dave's files, we ran across a transcript of a Texas Ranger report from 1878. The passage that caught our attention was about the arrest of some stage coach robbers near El Paso. "They are a part of the Kenny band who have been living in El Paso Mexico Dutch Marten Curly Bill and Buckskin Jo," the report declared.

After we reviewed the poorly written document, I asked Dave if he knew whether or not the man identified as Curly Bill was the same man of Tombstone fame. He wasn't sure if he was or not, and frankly, neither was I. After all, there must have been many men over the years who used the name Curly Bill. Still, because there were no books dedicated to Curly Bill Brocius, it was an intriguing mystery. We agreed that researching his life would be a worthwhile project, and after discussing the topic for a time, Dave handed the copy of the transcript to me to keep.

After leaving Dave's house, I drove thirty-six miles west to Crawfordsville, Indiana—the location of the leading theory about the hometown of William "Curly Bill" Brocius. I spent the entire day searching for information about Curly Bill. I checked the land records, the court documents, and the genealogical sources. My research into the notorious cowboy's life had begun. Of course, I was already knowledgable about Curly Bill, at least as well as some and probably more knowledgable than most. I had been researching John Ringo and Tombstone history for several years. At that time, I was reasonably confident that I could crack the riddle of Curly Bill's past in a relatively short time. During my visit to the town, I recognized that I could not corroborate the claim that Curly Bill was from Crawfordsville—or so I thought.

Around five o'clock that evening, I left the town and resumed my trip to Arizona. As I drove, my thoughts were on Curly Bill and his background. Yet, other matters took priority and I soon turned my attention to Ringo's past. My next stop was Gallatin, Missouri, a boyhood home of John Ringo. While researching for information on Ringo, I ran across a Brosius (spelled slightly different) family that had lived in the town. To my amazement, there was a William Brosius from the town, who had drifted to the West for a few years, but returned to Gallatin in 1883. Immediately, I wondered to myself whether he could be Curly Bill Brocius. After returning from the West, the man had settled down, studied medicine and became a medical doctor. Although the outlaw to doctor story was intriguing, I had a hard time believing it could be plausible that this man was Curly Bill Brocius.

I continued my journey to Arizona and, after spending a couple weeks there researching at the Arizona Historical Society and the University of Arizona library, started back to Michigan. While in Arizona, I had discovered that there was a William Brocius living in Henry County, Indiana, during 1860, and I decided to go there on my way back to Michigan to do some research. Henry County records indicated that there was a William Brosius, who also had a son named William, who had lived in the area.

Once I was back in Michigan, I started searching through indexes on genealogy. I soon realized that there was no shortage of men named William Brocius or Brosius (and there were other variations in the spelling as well) in Indiana. In fact, there were many men throughout the country with that name. It soon became a matter of eliminating from the potential Curly Bill candidates, the men who could not have been the famous outlaw. Some could be easily ruled out due to their age, but their census information still had to be reviewed because they may have had a son named William as well.

After a while, I realized that it would be extremely difficult to prove that any one man was Curly Bill Brocius because there was little, if any, way to prove a connection. It was quite clear that simply having the name William Brocius was not enough to establish a connection to Curly Bill. Compounding the problem was the claim that Curly Bill's real name was William Graham. Searching for records for the name William Brocius is difficult enough, but the name Graham is far too popular. In fact, there were more men named William Graham in the country than William Brocius. Some were even known to be living in Arizona, New Mexico, and Texas. Nevertheless, the same problem existed—how do you prove the connection between any one man to Curly Bill Brocius.

There are a number of people with the family name Brocius or Brosius who have claimed that, according to their family's legend, Curly Bill was one of their ancestors. Maybe so, but none seemed to have been able to provide any true evidence to locate his true name (and history) of the connection.

I decided that my search effort would be best served by backtracking Curly Bill, starting with the earliest documented record of him. Of course, that was the notorious cowboy's shooting of Tombstone Marshal Fred White. Still, there was the transcript of the Texas Ranger report from 1878 that stated a man named Curly Bill was arrested near El Paso. Moreover, after Wyatt Earp arrested Curly Bill in Tombstone for shooting White and transported the cowboy to the jail in Tucson, Earp told a *Tombstone Epitaph* reporter that Brocius had admitted that he was an escaped fugitive from El Paso.

After I had graduated from law school and had returned to Arizona, I started to make plans for a journey to El Paso to find Curly Bill. When I was able to get two weekdays free, I drove to El Paso to begin my research on his El Paso conviction. Once I arrived at the city, I stopped at the University of Texas at El Paso to look over microfilm copies of newspapers from the area. I discovered that the

El Paso Times, the newspaper that I was hoping to review, was not in print during 1878. Nevertheless, the *Mesilla Valley Independent*, a nearby town in New Mexico, was available. After loading the microfilm in the reader, I quickly began searching the newspaper for articles in late May 1878. Fortunately, there were a number of articles that discussed the robbery attempt and subsequent capture of Curly Bill. Yet, the articles did not use his real name. Only the sobriquet "Curly Bill" was used to described the suspected robber who was under arrest. The man arrested with him, who was named "Dutch Marten" in the Texas Ranger report of 1878, was identified as Bob Martin.

Toward the end of the day, I left the university and drove to the El Paso County Clerk's office, where I asked to see the criminal court docket from 1878. It was a huge book—most docket books are. Nevertheless, I anxiously scanned and flipped the pages of the docket book looking for the name William Brocius, but the name was not in the book. Fortunately, I did spot the name Robert Martin and directly below it was the name William Bresnaham—Curly Bill had used a different name.

The search for Curly Bill Brocius would be a hard one.

Steve Gatto
Lansing, Michigan

1

ALIAS CURLY BILL

On an October midnight in the year 1880, several men emerged from a Tombstone saloon on Allen Street with rowdy behavior on their minds and rotgut whiskey in their stomachs. As the group rambled down the dirt street looking for another bar to continue their party, and at a point near Allen Street and Sixth Street, a man in the group pulled out his six-gun and recklessly began "firing at the moon and stars."[1] The indiscriminate shooting, though not unusual in the silver boom town, caused a commotion in the street that quickly attracted the attention of the town's law officers. Almost immediately the men scattered, realizing that if they were found at the scene of the disturbance, being thrown in the town's jail for the night would abruptly end their painting the town.

Town Marshal Fred White, who was in the vicinity of Sixth Street and Allen Street when the gunfire erupted, responded to the shooting to prevent the "violation of city ordinance."[2] Also reacting to the gunshots was Pima County Deputy Sheriff Wyatt Earp. As a crowd of people rushed into the street to see what the commotion was about, White saw a man behind a building in a dark alley, and he rushed to apprehend him. The marshal announced he was an officer and demanded that the "suspect" give up his weapon. The man "put his hand behind him and commenced pulling the pistol" from its holster.[3] Once the gun was sufficiently free of the holster, Fred White "grabbed hold of the barrel" of the pistol. At the same moment, Wyatt Earp, who had just arrived at the scene, threw his arms around the man to see if he had any other weapons. Upon seeing deputy Earp there to assist him, Fred White said, "Now you G—d—s—of a b—give up that pistol;" and he "gave a quick jerk and the pistol went off."[4] With the gun now fully in his hands, White yelled, "I am shot" as he dropped the pistol and fell to the ground. He died two days later.[5]

Earp knocked the would-be assailant down, stepped over him and picked up the pistol. The deputy then grabbed the man by the collar and told him to get up. "What have I done? I have not done anything to be arrested for," the man protested.[6] Despite the man's plea of innocence, Earp arrested him and confined him in the city jail. The assailant was brought before Judge Michael Gray the next morning and charged with assault with intent to commit murder.[7] For the prisoner's safety, he was transported to Tucson because it was rumored that if White died, a vigilance committee would form to lynch him.[8] Following the marshal's death, the complaint was changed to murder.

The name of the man who was charged with the shooting of the town marshal was William Brocius, alias William Bresnaham, but soon to be known forever by the sobriquet "Curly Bill,"—cowboy, rustler, outlaw, and later, gang leader.[9] At the time of the shooting, Curly Bill, a cowboy from the San Simon area (about seventy miles northeast of Tombstone, near the New Mexico line) was not well known in Arizona.[10] Nonetheless, newspaper accounts of the incident published throughout the territory gave him instant notoriety as a man-killer. The *Tombstone Epitaph* added to his notoriety in the territory when it alleged that he was an escaped fugitive from Texas, who reportedly had "stopped a stage in El Paso County, Texas, killing one man and dangerously wounding another." [11] Like most of the cowboys—men who were generally considered rowdy and troublesome—it was presumed that he was from Texas. Yet, only his closest of friends may have known where he was from with any certainty.

Over the years several conflicting claims have been made concerning Curly Bill's background and name; yet none of these accounts inspires any real confidence regarding Curly's true lineage. An Arizona old-timer named Melvin Jones later wrote that Curly Bill was a "typical west Texas cowboy" whose real name was William Graham and that he had a brother named George.[12] According to Jones, "When Bill had to go on trial for the killing of Marshal White in

Tombstone, he gave the name of William Brocious."[13] Nevertheless, James C. Hancock, another pioneer, firmly denied that the notorious cowboy was known by the name Graham and, instead, asserted that Brocius grew up on the trail during cattle drives and that he never knew his parents.[14] About Melvin Jones' claim, Hancock wrote: "I was in Galeyville [Arizona] in 1881 and knew both the Grahams and also Curley Bill, and Bill Graham was one man and Curley Bill was another and they were not related."[15]

These contrasting old-timer claims, neither supported by any real evidence, have been relied upon by a number of writers since the 1920s to identify Curly Bill's true name. Thus, due in large part to the popularity of early books like Walter Noble Burns' *Tombstone: An Iliad of the Southwest* (1927) and Stuart Lake's *Wyatt Earp, Frontier Marshal* (1931), the name William Graham, whether correct or not, has now been inextricably intertwined with the saga of Curly Bill.[16] In fact, the possibility that Curly's real name was Graham has led to speculation that he may have been involved in the Lincoln County War in New Mexico. Some participants in this conflict, such as Dolly Graham, alias George Davis, alias Tom Jones, and others, were known to use the name Graham.[17] While there is no firm evidence linking the notorious cowboy to the New Mexico conflict, he provably did have an association with some of the men that participated in the feud.

Determined not to be overshadowed by the popularity that the name Graham has achieved in Tombstone lore, some people have attempted to preserve their infamous Tombstone namesake with accounts that declare that William Brocius was, indeed, Curly Bill's real name. For example, one claimant insists, categorically and without corroboration, that Curly Bill was an ancestor of his and that the notorious cowboy's real name was William Brocius.[18] This informant asserts that Curly Bill was a prosperous uncle who did not die until well after the turn of the century. According to this account, the Brocius family preferred to remain anonymous in order to allow would-be searchers for Curly Bill's past to continue to stumble around in the dark without any real clues about his background. Unfortunately, the claimant's anonymity diminishes the account's overall credibility.

More recently, a "supposed" descendent declared that Tombstone's most famous outlaw was from Indiana.[19] This claim states that William Brocius, prior to gaining notoriety in Arizona, was a poor dirt farmer from Crawfordsville, Indiana. According to the story, Brocius accepted money from another man to take his place as an enlistee in the Union Army. Following the cessation of fighting in the war, Brocius did not return to Indiana for almost five years. When he finally did show up, he found that his wife, who believed that her tardy husband was killed in battle, had remarried. He reportedly left the town an angry man who was never heard from again.

Unlike the anonymous ancestor's story, this account does provide facts and names to bolster the credibility of the account. Nonetheless, the information is prone to error and does not provide any real proof that this William Brocius was Tombstone's Curly Bill Brocius.[20] Instead, the story proclaims that "he left town an angry man and was never heard from again."[21] If this man had left Indiana in 1869 and was never heard from again, how could anyone know whether he was the same man who became famous in Arizona? Simply having the same name is not enough to establish a connection between the two men. Provably, there were dozens of men scattered throughout the United States during this period that had the name William Brocius.[22]

Other accounts, rather than simply settling on the name of Brocius or Graham, interchange the two names by asserting that one was his mother's maiden name. One dubious claim asserts that Curly Bill's real name was William Brocius Graham, and that his parents were George Benjamin Graham and Sarah (Brocius) Graham of Gonzales, Texas.[23] Yet, no contemporary evidence supporting the account has been found.[24] Without further documentation or supporting evidence, this claim and many others like it lack substantiation. Regardless of what his true name was, most people knew him simply as "Curly Bill."

Curly Bill left no letters or writings that provided clues to his life before Tombstone. An Arizona newspaper in 1881 claimed that the nefarious cowboy was twenty-five years old (suggesting a birthdate around 1856) and from Texas.[25] However, it is impossible at this point to check the accuracy of the report. William Breakenridge, who was a deputy sheriff in Tombstone, later provided a description of the cowboy that is generally accepted by historians: "fully six feet tall, with black, curly hair, freckled face and well built."[26] Some rumors mention that his complexion was a little dark—suggesting a trace of Mexican or possibly African bloodlines.[27] However, no real facts have been found to prove the validity of these claims either. No documented photographs are known to exist of Curly Bill.[28] Likewise, no details about Curly Bill's mother or father survive. Perhaps his parents died while he was young (as one account suggests) and he simply drifted toward a life of outlawry. Without more information, where or when Curly Bill was born—or even his true name—remains a mystery.

Wyatt Earp provided the best clue to the infamous cowboy's life before Tombstone. After delivering Brocius to the county jail in Tucson, Earp returned the next day to Tombstone. Upon arriving back home, Wyatt reported some things that he had learned about the mysterious stranger who shot Fred White. The October 31, 1880, *Tombstone Epitaph* gave its readers a summary of Earp's findings:

> From Deputy Sheriff Earp we learn that the man who killed Marshal White is an old offender against the law. Within the past few years he stopped a stage in El Paso County, Texas, killing one man and dangerously wounding another. He was tried and sentenced to the penitentiary, but managed to make his escape shortly after being incarcerated. The facts leaked out in this way: On the road to Tucson, Byoscins [Brocius] asked Earp where he could get a good lawyer. Earp suggested that Hereford & Zabriskie were considered a good firm. Broscins [Brocius] said that he didn't want Zabriskie, as he had prosecuted him once in Texas. Inquiry on the part of Earp developed the above state of facts.

Curly Bill's carefree but foolish admission to deputy Earp of his escape from El Paso two years earlier could have created drastic consequences for the desperado. It is quite likely that Earp made inquiries to Texas authorities concerning an escaped man named William Brocius. If the lawman did seek out information, either none was returned or no record of a man named Brocius could be found; Curly Bill had used the name William Bresnaham in Texas when he was convicted in 1878.[29] However, the convicted felon was also known by the name Curly Bill at the time of his conviction and a hard-nosed court clerk with a good memory might have realized that Brocius was the same man. Yet, the man later dubbed "Arizona's most famous outlaw" had a different destiny to follow than to be returned to a Texas jail.[30] More importantly, Curly Bill's use of the name Bresnaham in 1878 further confuses the issue regarding the cowboy's true name. Indeed, since this is the first documented name used by Curly Bill, it could also be argued that Bresnaham was his true name and that Brocius was an alias that he assumed after escaping from Texas.

The charge against Curly Bill for killing Fred White was dismissed by a judge in Tucson on December 27, 1880.[31] Despite the court's legal decision that the shooting was an accident, many people maintained the Curly Bill had intentionally murdered Tombstone Town Marshal Fred White.[32] Following his release from the Pima County jail, Curly Bill's activities remained the focus of public attention throughout the territory. During January 1881, the cowboy wreaked havoc in the small communities of Charleston and Contention City on consecutive weeks.[33] Rumors of "grave outrages" like making people dance at gunpoint and shooting out gaslights, spread throughout the territory.[34] In a short time, the cowboy was perceived by the public as the leader of a band of desperadoes.

Still, the cowboy's notorious reputation in Arizona had its beginnings with the killing of Fred White in Tombstone. No matter where he was from or what name he used, he would forever be remembered as "'Curly Bill,' the man who murdered Fred White in Tombstone."[35]

2

ON THE ROAD TO MESILLA

Two years earlier, toward the end of May 1878, Curly Bill was spending time in El Paso, Texas, and in the Mexican town of El Paso Del Norte, "the pass of the North," presumably getting drunk and being rowdy.[1] The cowboy reportedly was part of a group of desperadoes whose presence in the area was creating considerable tension amongst the local authorities. "There is a mob of outlaws located round El Paso Texas & Mexico that threaten us with trouble," wrote Lieutenant J. A. Tays of the Texas Rangers in a letter dated May 16, 1878.[2] Five days later, Tays' fear of trouble materialized with a botched attempted robbery of a government wagon.

On the afternoon of May 21, 1878, Lieutenant Benjamin Butler and two "Buffalo Soldiers" from the 9th Cavalry left El Paso for Mesilla, New Mexico, in a government ambulance. After the military wagon had traveled about eight miles, two men, later identified as Curly Bill and Bob Martin, passed them on the road. At a bend in the road, the two men, now wearing masks, sprang from the bushes near the roadside, ordered the driver to halt, and opened fire on the men in the wagon. A bullet hit the driver in the shoulder, inflicting a serious wound. The other soldier also was shot , "one ball penetrating his right lung, another entering his stomach and a third lodging in his right thigh."[3] Lt. Butler grabbed a carbine rifle, jumped to the ground, and commenced to fire at the attackers.

After a brief exchange of gunfire, Curly Bill and Bob Martin fled through the brush and made their escape. A short time after the robbery attempt, five Texas Rangers arrived at the scene. The *Mesilla Valley Independent*, on May 23, 1878, published an exciting account of the attack:

Tuesday the 21st, inst., was a field day for the Banditti; about four o'clock on the afternoon of that day, a government ambulance containing Lieut. Benj. I. Butler of the 9th Cavalry, and two soldiers of the same Regiment, while en-route from El Paso to Mesilla, was overtaken and passed near White's Ranche, eight miles north of El Paso, by two masked men, one of whom is said to be the notorious "Bob Martin." About two miles further on, at a bend in the road, these same men, masked, sprang from the bushes near the road and ordered the driver to halt, simultaneously with the demand they both opened fire on the men in the ambulance. The driver was struck in the shoulder the ball passing out near his spine inflicting a serious wound, the other soldier Johnson [sic] of Co. "G," 9th cavalry was hit three times one ball penetrating his right lung, another entered his stomach and a third lodged in his right thigh, inflicting at least one mortal wound. As the wounded men fell back in the ambulance; Lieut. Butler grasped a carbine from the hands of one of them and sprang to the ground, whereupon the cowardly assassins fled through the brush and made their escape. Corporal Mathews with four men of the Texas Rangers came up shortly afterwards and followed the trail of the murderers to the River and discovered that they had crossed into Mexico. The wounded men were taken back to El Paso Texas where they now lie in a critical condition. The object of the attack was undoubtedly robbery, it being supposed that Lieut. Butler had a considerable sum of money about his person. Lieutenant Butler reached this place about noon to-day (Wednesday.) The ambulance is riddled with bullets and stained with the blood of the wounded men.

The Texas Rangers trailed the two bandits until it became apparent to the lawmen that the outlaws had crossed into Mexico. Lieutenant Butler took the wounded soldiers back to El Paso, and their arrival in the border town caused a great deal of commotion. Two additional stage robberies around this time helped to fuel the excitement in the town. The two desperadoes, now in Mexico, thought they were safe from arrest, but they were mistaken. The following day, on May 22, 1878, Mexican authorities in "Paseo Del Norte" arrested Bob Martin and "Curley" and offered to hold them for extradition. When the news that the Mexican police had the outlaws under arrest reached the army post, the military officers quickly paid $75 for their capture:

> Latest From El Paso.
>
> Attempted Murderers of Lt. Butler
> and party Captured.
>
>   El Paso, May 23, 1878.
> Bob Martin and a man known as "Curley" were arrested in El Paso, Mexico, last evening charged with being the parties who attempted to murder Leut Butler and party near Whites ranche on Monday last. "Buckskin Joe" was also arrested, although he was not with the party at the time the attack was made, but one of the robbers rode his horse, and had his arms. The Mexican authorities offer to hold the parties for extradition. The Military officers at the Post paid $75 for their capture. The wounded soldier died today.[4]

Mexican authorities delivered Curly Bill and Bob Martin to military officers, who confined the two desperadoes in the nearby military prison at Franklin.[5] Sometime later the county sheriff took custody of the two men, but, rather than holding them in El Paso, he took them to the Texas Rangers at Ysleta, where they were incarcerated at the Rangers' quarters. There was no real jail at Ysleta that could safely house the prisoners. Instead, at night the prisoners were often chained to stakes in the yard. During the day, if it was warm, the prisoners remained outside in the yard, but when the weather was cold the prisoners were placed in a long, dark room. Under these conditions of confinement, Curly Bill and Bob Martin remained for the next five months.[6]

In a poorly written report about the incident to Major John B. Jones, Tays identified Curly Bill and Bob Martin as members of Kinney's gang that had been living around El Paso:

> Ysleta El Paso Texas
> May 31 1878
> To J. B. Jones
> Maj. Comd. Frot. Batt.
>
> Sir
> On the 20 I received information that Indians had shot the mail cariers 15 miles above Franklin and ware raiding in the Canutea bottom I sent Sgt Ryal and five men to scout in that locality They met Lt B. I. Butler who was on his way home and had been attact by robers only a few minutes before and his driver and escort shot himself narrowly escaping Sgt Ryal gave him a man to assist in taking the wounded men to a house and he and the rest went after the robers and chased them until they crossed the river into Mexico and had the robers arrested They are a part of the Kenny band who have been living in El Paso Mexico Dutch Marten Curly Bill and Buckskin Jo The authorities gave them over to the Military who have them up on trial before W. B. Blanshard who is the new justice for Franklin Hague is defending them.
>
> J.A. Tays [7]

Five months earlier, Kinney and his band, which likely included Curly Bill and Bob Martin, had come to the area from Silver City, New Mexico, to participate in the bloody El Paso Salt War.[8] The Salt War was a bitter racial conflict that pitted Texan against Mexican and probably had more to do with politics and personal conflicts than salt deposits at the foot of Guadalupe Peak, located 100 miles east of El Paso.[9] The conflict had its beginnings two months before the arrival of Kinney and his men, when growing antagonism in the area caused Major John B. Jones of the Texas Rangers to organize a detachment at San Elizario, twenty miles east of El Paso. A month later the situation climaxed when a Mexican mob killed two men at San Elizario and then besieged Charles Howard at the Texas Rangers' quarters. On the fifth day of the siege, Howard gave himself up and the Rangers surrendered, believing that the mob would not harm Howard. Nevertheless, a Mexican firing squad shot Howard and two other men. The mob mutilated Howard's body with machetes and then dragged the three corpses for a short distance before throwing the lifeless bodies into an old well. The Rangers left San Elizario in disgrace without their weapons, and the mob looted the town.[10]

When news of the San Elizario incident and a call for help from El Paso Sheriff Charles Kerber reached Silver City, New Mexico, John Kinney and several other men responded. They formed a "Company of Volunteers of State Forces."[11] The volunteers were commanded by Lieutenant Dan Tucker, a deputy sheriff of Grant County, New Mexico. The volunteers, or "Silver City Rangers" as they were called, rode to Texas and were attached to federal troops and a company of Texas Rangers.[12] The combined force then proceeded to San Elizario. In the ensuing confrontation, at least four Mexicans were killed and a few others wounded in retribution by Kinney's band of New Mexico volunteers, which was reputedly made up of several men with unsavory backgrounds. Fearing more retaliation from Americans, the leaders of the Mexican mob and many of their followers fled to Mexico.[13]

The Company of Volunteers of State Forces was disbanded around January 10, 1878, but John Kinney and many of his men remained in the El Paso area for several months, providing a new and much different threat of trouble.

One of the most notorious members of Kinney's band was Bob Martin, who was well known in southern New Mexico and western Texas. He was suspected in a number of crimes involving John Kinney and the Jesse Evans gang in New Mexico. The outlaw had been indicted a year earlier in Dona Ana County, New Mexico, for stealing cattle but was never arrested on the charge.[14] About Martin's criminal past, the *Mesilla Valley Independent* wrote: "There are several indictments against Martin in the U.S. and Territorial Courts of this country for stage robbery, larceny, etc., and should he escape the punishment he so richly merits in Texas we ask to have him sent up here...."[15] Compared to Martin, Curly Bill was just starting to gain a notorious reputation in the area, and only his sobriquet was used by newspapers in articles that discussed the incident.

In June 1878, Kinney and his men left the El Paso area for Lincoln County, New Mexico, where they participated in the Lincoln County War. Meanwhile, Curly Bill and Bob Martin, who were still in custody in Texas, tried to free themselves from the custody of the Texas Rangers. The *Mesilla News*, on July 13, 1878, reported the result of the escape attempt:

> Our friend S. Schutz the obliging Postmaster at El Paso has been up this way buying good of Spiegelberg Bros. He informs us that "Curley" and Bob Martin succeeded in filing the irons off themselves while in confinement, and at a favorable opportunity made a desperate attempt to escape, but were recaptured before they had gone 200 yards, returned to their quarters and secured more firmly. If they should be permitted to escape it would be a shame and disgrace. Put them through.

Two months following their failed escape attempt, on September 2, 1878, the El Paso County sheriff and a Texas Ranger escorted Curly Bill and Bob Martin to Franklin for their appearances before the district court.[16] The *Mesilla Valley Independent* commented: "Martin and Curly Bill [were to be tried] for highway robbery and attempt to kill Lt. Butler and escort."[17] Case number 300—Robert Martin et al was filed on September 6, 1878, in the El Paso County court docket.[18] The court records finally revealed Curly Bill's full name, at least the name he was using at the time—William Bresnaham. Two and a half years later he used the name William Brocius in Tombstone after being arrested for shooting Marshal Fred White, and he became well known in Arizona and the Southwest as "Curly Bill Brocius." [19]

Doc Holliday, a friend of Wyatt Earp and participant in the now famous 1881 "Gunfight at the OK Corral" in Tombstone, Arizona, told a reporter from the *Denver Republican* in 1882 that Curly Bill Brocius was the man involved in the attack on the government ambulance: " The Curly Bill mentioned by Mallen [a man who arrested Holliday in Colorado] was a most notorious character wanted by the United States for a number of outrages, among which were the killing of the El Paso marshal and the shooting of Lieutenant Butler, a son of General B. F. Butler, during an attempted stagecoach robbery." [20] No corroborating evidence that Curly killed an El Paso marshal has been found. However, Lieutenant Butler, who was one of the men attacked but not shot during the holdup attempt, was the son of General Benjamin Franklin Butler, known as "Beast" or "Spoons Butler." General Butler received these pejorative nicknames as a result of his controversial command of the occupying forces in New Orleans during the Civil War.[21]

In El Paso County, when being indicted by the grand jury for assault with intent to kill Charles Johnston and George Shakespear during the attack on the government ambulance, Curly Bill was referred to as William Bresnaham:

> Robert Martin & William Bresnaham on the 24th day [actually the 21st] of the month of May A. D. 1878, in the county of El Paso and State of Texas did then and

there in and upon Charles Johnston and George
Shakespear unlawfully feloniously make an assault
with intent then the said Charles Johnston & George
Shakespear then & there unlawfully, feloniously,
willfully, & their malice aforethought to kill and murder,
against the peace & dignity of the State.
J. K. Ball
Foreman of Grand Jury [22]

On September 12, 1878, the State of Texas tried Curly Bill
and Bob Martin, who were jointly indicted for assault with intent to
murder. The following court document explains what happened:

The State of Texas   )
No. 300 vs   ) On the 12th
Robert Martin and   ) day of September A.D. 1878
William Bresnaham) came on to be heard
& for trial the above no. & entitled cause, & the State
of Texas & each of said Defendants announced ready
for Trial, whereupon came a jury of twelve qualified
Jurors, to wit: George Zwitzers—and eleven others
who were duly sworn according to the law in said
cause & who heard the indictment read & defendants
Robt. Martin & William Bresnaham each pleaded not
guilty & said jury after hearing all the evidence,
argument of Counsel & the Charge of the Court retired
to consider of this verdict after due consideration
returned into open & for their verdict say and present
to the court their verdict as follows: to wit . . .

We the jury in the aforesaid cases find the parties
guilty & assess the punishment at five years penitentiary.
Geo. Zwitzers
Foreman

The State prays that the above entry be made minus
pro time & that the records stands as so amended.
T. A. Fahey
Dist. Atty pro tem [23]

The judge sentenced William "Curly Bill" Bresnaham and
Robert Martin to five years in the state prison, minus the time that they
had already served in jail waiting for their trial. Two days following
their sentencing, on September 14, 1878, the law firm of James &
Carpenter filed, on behalf of the two convicted men, a motion for a
new trial, citing four issues:

> 1st Because a material witness of the Defts was
> prevented from attending the Court at the trial of Defts
> by threats.

> 2nd Because the verdict is contrary to the laws & the
> evidence and not in accordance with the charge of
> the court.

> 3rd Because the verdict does not decide the issue
> between the parties or assess any punishment
> prescribed by the laws of Texas.

> 4th Because the verdict is too vague uncertain and
> indefinite to support a judgement of sentence.

James & Carpenter
Attys for Defts [24]

On September 16, Paul W. Keating, a Texas Ranger, signed
a sworn affadivit stating that he had gone to Mexico at the request of
the defendants' attorneys to obtain the presence of a witness who
wanted to testify in their behalf at their trial, but the witness was afraid
to appear at the court due to threats he had received:

This day personally appeared before me the undersigned authority Paul W. Keating who be duly sworn states that the affiant at the request of the attys of the Defts Robert Martin & William Bresnaham went to the town of El Paso Mexico for the purpose of obtaining the attendance of Joseph Jerald as a witness at the trial of said Deft Robert Martin and William Bresnaham in case No 300 in the District Court of El Paso County Texas September term 1878 as a witness in behalf of said Defts. that affiant saw the said Joseph Jerald and stated the object of his visit and the said Jerald expressed a willingness to attend at the trial of said cause as such witness but was afraid to do so because he had been threatened & notified by the Jeffe-politica and other Mexican authorities of El Paso Mexico that if he the said Jerald did attend said trial as such witness that he would have to leave the Country because Joseph Jerald was only taking the part of the said defendants because they are Americans the said Jerald stated to the affiant that he saw the said Deft Martin at about four o clock in the afternoon of the 24th day of May 1878 in front of the store of Peter Dyce in the town of El Paso Mexico and conversed with him and that said Martin was at that time carrying horse feed on his horse.

Paul W. Keating

Sworn to and Subscribed to before me this 16th day of September 1878.

GW Wahl [25]

The chief argument raised by the appellate team was that a material witness for the defense was prevented from testifying due to threats made against him. Joe Jerald was prepared to testify that he had seen Bob Martin on "May 24" [actually May 21], around four o'clock "in front of the store of Peter Dyce in the town of El Paso,

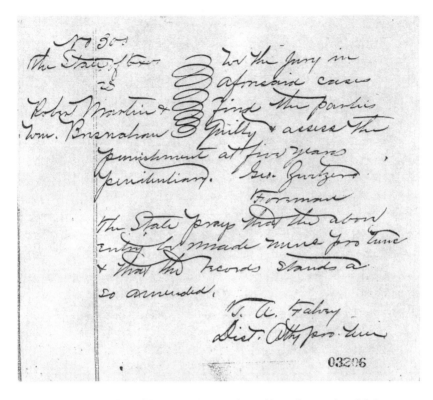

A jury found Curly Bill and Bob Martin guilty of assault with intent to murder and their punishment was assessed at five years in the penitentiary. El Paso County Court Clerk's Office, El Paso, Texas

Docket entry showing that Curly Bill was using the name William Bresnaham at the time of his arrest and conviction in 1878.
El Paso County Court Clerk's Office, El Paso, Texas

Mexico." [26] This would have provided Martin with an alibi. Unfortunately, Jerald claimed he did not appear in court the day of the trial because "he had been threatened by the 'Jeffe Politica' [chief government official] and other Mexican authorities" and that if he did attend the trial as a defense witness "he would have to leave the country." [27]

Curly Bill and Bob Martin, while waiting for the results of the appeal, remained in custody at Ysleta, being guarded by Texas Rangers. "The two prisoners charged with intent to kill Lt. Butler and guard have been on trial and sentenced to five years [in] the Penintentiary, but they are arguing for a [new] trial," wrote Lt. James Tays to Major John B. Jones. [28] During mid-September, Kinney and his men had returned to El Paso after fighting in the Lincoln County War in New Mexico. "Kinney has made his appearance again with quite a strong party but they are operating on the Mexican side of the river," wrote James Tays to Major Jones. [29]

During the evening of November 2, 1878, Curly Bill, Bob Martin, and three Mexican prisoners made a successful escape from the jail. They quickly headed for Mexico, crossing the Rio Grande River later that night. Tays provided Major Jones an explanation of the escape of the prisoners in his custody:

> I am sorry to inform you that the prisoners we have
> been guarding made their escape on the Evening of
> the Second Nov. by digging under the wall and they
> had their Shackels cut off they leaving the saws and
> other tools behind them We missed them ten minutes
> after they left but dark coming on we could not find
> them The next morning found their tracks going a
> cross the river . . . . [30]

Possibly expecting criticism for the escape, Tays was quick to place blame elsewhere: "I blame the negligence of the Sheriff in not providing suitable fisctures [sic] and not seeing that we had a suitable room to keep prisoners of their character in . . . ." [31] A local resident,

Bryan Callaghan, apparently agreed with Tays' assessment that they lacked the proper facilities to hold real desperadoes for any length of time. In a letter to Major Jones, dated December 9, 1878, Callaghan wrote: "The escape of the Mexican prisoners at Ysleta I attribute to two Americans who had been convicted and sentenced to five years in the State Penitentiary; and such jail birds cannot hardly be kept in the best jails of the State—Ysleta has no jail as you know." [32]

Curly Bill and Bob Martin successfully evaded recapture by Texas authorities. For the next two years their whereabouts were seemingly unknown, although Martin was occassionally mentioned in newspapers or personal correspondence regarding livestock theft in Mexico. The wanted Texas felons likely roamed from Mexico to New Mexico and Arizona. By 1880 both men were known to be headquartered in the San Simon Valley, an area that stretched across the Arizona and New Mexico borders and was home to a thriving community of desperadoes.

Govenor John C. Fremont informed Carl Schurz, the Secretary of the Interior, that Robert Martin's gang numbered about one hundred and twenty. Cowboy Depredations File, Record Group 60, National Archives, Washington D.C.

3

ROBERT MARTIN GANG

After escaping from Texas authorities, Bob Martin and Curly Bill fled to Mexico to avoid being recaptured. However, within a month the two fugitives likely stole sixty-eight head of cattle from northern Chihuahua and drove the herd into New Mexico.[1] Curly Bill's whereabouts and his activities for the next two years are not known with certainty. Nevertheless, Bob Martin, Curly's former jail mate, was occasionally mentioned during this period in newspapers and increasingly in government correspondence as a leader of a gang of outlaws raiding across the Mexican border into the states of Sonora and Chihuahua and stealing livestock.[2] Although Curly Bill received no attention in any correspondence and no public notoriety in connection with Bob Martin's activities after their escape from Texas, it is likely that Brocius participated in at least some of Martin's border excursions.

During the outlaws' incarceration in Texas, Mexican officials had learned and reported that desperadoes in Arizona were raiding across the Mexican border stealing livestock. "Bands have been formed in Arizona which cross the Mexican frontier, in the district of El Setar. They steal horses in Arizona which they come to sell in Mexico, where they also steal cattle which they drive off to sell in Arizona. They commit all sorts of crimes," protested a Mexican official in December 1878.[3] It was only natural that wanted Texas felons like Bob Martin and Curly Bill should make their way to Arizona and, once there, quickly blend in with other so-called cowboys. They eventually settled in the

San Simon Valley, an area that stretched between Arizona and New Mexico and was home to a thriving community of outlaws and desperadoes. The area was perfect for ranching, providing easy access to the markets for livestock in both Arizona and New Mexico, and a short distance to towns in Mexico. In addition, a railroad depot was established at the town of San Simon during 1880, which brought with it another possible outlet for the distribution of livestock. Nonetheless, while the San Simon Valley was ideal for ranching and distribution of livestock, the remote location was particularly suited for criminal activity. Bandits used the Mexican border to their advantage, raiding on one side and finding safe haven on the other.

There were several factions of men commonly referred to as "cowboys" that roamed throughout the area. Some of these men, like Charles Ray, "alias Pony Deal or Diehl," were known outlaws before arriving in Arizona.[4] Pony Deal was a veteran of the Lincoln County War, a probable participant in the El Paso Salt War, and a suspected cattle thief and murderer. In contrast, Sherman McMasters was a Texas Ranger before coming to Arizona. In fact, Bob Martin and Curly Bill escaped from McMasters' Ranger detachment in Ysleta, Texas, during November 1878.[5] In the West, however, it was not uncommon for a man to be a law officer in one place and an outlaw in the next. Together, Deal and McMasters were accused of holding up at least one stage in Arizona. In July 1880, "Pony Diehl, A. T. Hansbrough, and Mac Demasters," probably Sherman McMasters, were publicly accused of stealing six government mules from Camp Rucker (located in the Chiricahua Mountains forty miles east of Tombstone).[6] Although Curly Bill was not publicly implicated in the crime at the time, writers occasionally have included him, without corroboration, in the theft of the six government mules.[7]

Other men seem to have come to the area to work as miners before turning to a life of outlawry. Will and Milt Hicks were apparently miners in Grant County, New Mexico, for a time.[8] However, the brothers, who possibly associated with Curly Bill, both were charged in 1881 with cattle theft before leaving Arizona to avoid arrest.[9] William Grounds, alias "Billy the Kid," also started out in the New Mexico town of Shakespeare working as a miner in 1880, but he too soon changed vocations.[10] Grounds later was suspected of criminal activity and was indicted for cattle theft in November 1881, along with Curly Bill Brocius, "Led" Moore, and Zwing Hunt, another transplanted Texan.[11] William Tettenbaum, alias Russian Bill, a thirty-year-old immigrant from Russia, likewise started out in the Shakespeare district as a miner in 1880.[12] A little over a year later, during November 1881, Russian Bill and another would-be cowboy hard case, Sandy King, were lynched by vigilantes in the mining town of Shakespeare.[13]

Some cowboys, like Dick Lloyd, though somewhat rowdy and reckless while drinking whiskey, came to Arizona driving cattle and stayed in the area working on ranches, presumably as honest cowboys. Men such as John Ringo and Joe Hill had participated in deadly feuds like the Hoodoo War in Texas and left that state after the violence subsided.[14] Ike Clanton, together with his brothers Phineas and William and his father, Newman H. Clanton, had moved to Arizona in 1873.[15] Although most of the family later resided near Charleston, Ike had made the move to the San Simon Valley by 1880.[16] In November 1880, Ike Clanton and John Ringo established a 320-acre ranch in the Animas Valley.[17]

Yet, before many of these men arrived in Arizona, Bob Martin and his men, who likely included Curly Bill, were moving livestock from Mexico to New Mexico and Arizona. In January 1879, Indian contractor E. F. Walz made the following comments about the nefarious business and the role of Bob Martin, who now was considered a leader of a band of thieves:

> I have a heard [sic] of Cattle on the road from Sullivan's Ranch in the State of Chihuahua en route to the San Carlos Agency [in Arizona] to be delivered to the Indians. The herd consists of 800 to 400 beef steers. I am just informed that there

are some hostile Indians on the route which goes
by the Hatchet Mountains and San Simon [.] Also
I am informed that quite a band of thieves under
Bob Martin the man who shot Lt. Butler have
threatented and are preparing to stampede my herd.
I request that an escort or scout be sent to meet
said herd at the Hatchet Mountains and escort them
to the point of crossing the Arizona line. The herd
is under the charge of John H. Riley.[18]

A month later, reports of Americans stealing cattle in
Chihuahua near Janos and taking them north "to be incorporated
and crossed at the first opportunity to the United States" began to
spread from Mexico.[19] "The presence of Martin in that section
and the frequency with which robberies have been committed in
New Mexico and Texas near the dividing line keeps the inhabitants
in the greatest alarm," noted one report.[20] Mexican officials sent
offical complaints about Americans stealing cattle in Chihuahua,
but no action from government officials in Washington was
forthcoming. In September 1879, Martin was noted to be "lurking"
in New Mexico between Silver City and Las Cruces and "with a
mixed band of white men & Mexicans has been attacking cattle &
horses in Corralitos, Casas Inandas, & that section and running
them into Arizona & New Mexico."[21]
        Once livestock was brought to the United States, it was
difficult, if not impossible, to recover the stock because alleged
crimes in Mexico were not crimes in the United States. Moreover,
American ranchers quickly bought the Mexican livestock at low
prices to build their herds, and middlemen found contractors eager
to fill government orders or furnished meat to local towns.[22] The
Mexicans' only real recourse for the theft of cattle or horses was
to forcibly take back the stolen livestock. Of course, it was also
necessary for Americans to use the same self-help methods to
regain livestock stolen by Mexicans. This appears to have been
the situation along the Arizona and New Mexico border. Often

gun battles would be waged before one party or the other would retreat.

When allegations of cowboy offenses in Arizona and Mexico finally reached Arizona Governor John C. Fremont, he was greatly surprised to hear that "bands of robbers" were organized in Arizona.[23] At the time, Fremont was under the impression that Mexican bandits, like Brigido Reyes, were mainly responsible for the problems occurring in the area.[24] However, by January 1881, the Governor finally accepted the apparent existence of Robert Martin's band of outlaws, which he estimated numbered about one hundred and twenty.[25] Although Curly Bill likely participated in some of the Bob Martin's raids, it appears he received little, if any, public attention for his role in the crimes.

During June 1880, additional complaints from the Mexican government were made to the Secretary of State of the United States. "A bandit by profession who for some time past has been marauding on both frontiers, has succeeded in forming a gang of Texans and Mexicans who at present have taken refuge in Sierra del Hache in American territory from whence they separate to commit their depredations, stealing large numbers of cattle, which pass on that side of the frontier," indicated one report.[26]

At some point it appears that Bob Martin was captured by Mexican authorites, but a district judge freed him. "If the outlaw Martin, who is the leader of these Texans, had not been unjustly acquitted, we should now be at peace; though Martin was arrested by order of the Government, he was protected by the District Judge, and we, whose blood is now being shed, are today suffering the fatal consequences of that protection," wrote Juan M. Zuloaga, the Governor of Chihuahua.[27] Curly Bill may also have been captured but later released. In 1883, the *El Paso Daily Times* alleged that Curly Bill had also been arrested around this time largely due to the effort of Tom Mode, a member of Major George B. Zimpleman's Guards that formed "to break up the bands of cattle thieves and murderers infesting the pastoral regions" of Texas:

It was while in the latter hazardous business that he [Mode] became one of the most conspicuous actors in the first capture of the notorious 'Curly Bill' . . . . In company with several of the guards he succeeded in corraling the desperate outlaw and some of his men in a cabin, where a fight to the death began. Mode in his reckless disregard of danger was marked as a target by the robber chief. But while in the act of leveling his gun, Curly Bill exposed the side of his face at the window, when the quick aim of Mode sent a ball crashing through that cut the right ear off and laid the villian out insensible. This virtually ended the fight and broke up the gang.[28]

In August 1880, possibly four or five men in Martin's gang were killed and others wounded in clashes with Mexican citizens and Zimpleman's Guards near San Luis and Corralitos.[29] A Silver City newspaper article suggested that one of the wounded men may have been Curly Bill: "Rogers, or Curly Bill, was accidentally shot at San Simon on Sunday last. Dr. Henry Woodville will leave on the coach in the mornng to attend him."[30] The next day, the newspaper clarified how Curly Bill was really injured: "That accident noticed yesterday as having occurred at San Simon, turns out to have been a regular battle between some 4 or 5 Americans and about 40 Mexicans, over some cattle that were claimed to have been stolen."[31] Was Rogers, in actuality, Curly Bill Brocius?[32] One old-timer later told of a similar incident involving Curly Bill, in which he had been shot during a border raid by Mexicans but made it back to New Mexico to be treated by a doctor:

Once when the Mexicans went after the gang, Curly Bill got separated from the rest and the Mexicans shot him in the butt, but did not hit a bone. Bill rode over 200 miles to Lordsburg to see a doctor.[33]

If Brocius was shot in August 1880, the wound was not too serious and he mended quickly. During October 1880, the cowboy and three others reportedly "treed" [tormented and harassed for fun] San Simon. "On Monday night four cow-boys took San Simon by storm, and, by dint of firing their revolvers, were in full possession, having chased everybody out. One of the S. P. R. R. engineers was forced to take to the brush leaving his engine in their hands; but as the fire was out, they could not use it." [34] Curly Bill's next shooting spree toward the end of October in Tombstone would end with a much different result.

Bob Martin was shot in the head and killed near Stein's Pass in the San Simon Valley on November 22, 1880.[35] Ironically, Bob Martin, the man proclaimed to be the leader of 120 cowboys, was killed by a gang of four rustlers.

CURLY BILL

Curly Bill's shooting of Marshal Fred White in Tombstone gave the cowboy instant notoriety in the territory as a desperate man-killer. Illustration of Curly Bill courtesy Bob Boze Bell.

4

THE MURDEROUS PISTOL

In late October 1880, about two weeks following the "treeing" of the San Simon train depot and attempt to hijack a locomotive, Curly Bill and some friends rode to Tombstone, a distance of seventy-five miles. At the silver boom town, their rowdy and boisterous behavior created much concern among the townspeople. "A company of five cow-boys . . . have been carousing about town for several days and boasting that if our officers interfered with them they would eat them, as they frequently dined on officers," noted the *Arizona Daily Star*.[1] Just after midnight, on October 28, 1880, the town's worst fear became a reality, with a deadly result.

Tombstone's origins date back to 1877 when Ed Schieffelin discovered a rich silver lode in southeastern Arizona. In 1878, after hearing of Schieffelin's silver discoveries, hopeful prospectors trekked to the Tombstone district. First a haphazard collection of tents, the camp grew rapidly, and more substantial buildings were constructed. The Pima County Board of Supervisors incorporated Tombstone as a "village" in November 1879, and the first local election took place on November 24. William Harwood won the contest for mayor and Fred White was elected town marshal. The regular municipal election took place on January 6, 1880; Alder Randall became mayor, and Fred White retained his position as town marshal.

A month earlier, around December 1, 1879, former Dodge City lawman Wyatt Earp and his common-law wife, Celia Ann "Mattie" Blaylock, slowly drove their wagon into Tombstone.[2] In two other wagons rode Wyatt's older brothers, Virgil and James, and their wives, Allie and Bessie. Morgan Earp and his wife, Louisa, would come to town a few months later. Contrary to popular legend, when Wyatt first came to Arizona, he did not have a prominent reputation stemming from his Dodge City days, and his name was unknown to the average citizen in southern Arizona. Before leaving Prescott, the territorial capital, Virgil Earp was appointed deputy United States marshal by U.S. Marshal Crawley Dake.[3]

On October 27, 1880, several cowboys, likely including Curly Bill, were in Tombstone, when a bucking and kicking colt at Brown's corral attracted their attention. The cowboys gathered around the corral, and Dick Lloyd volunteered to ride the colt. With "a big crowd gathered to see the fun," the cowboy broke the horse to the delight of the onlookers.[4] Sometime after Lloyd's "tall bucking," Curly Bill and several others, including cowboy Dick Lloyd, rancher Frank Patterson, Ed Collins, Andrew Ames, and Charleston miner James Johnson, began drinking in Thomas Corrigan's saloon on Allen Street.[5] Later in the evening, the group was joined by Andrew McCauley, a Tombstone resident for the past two years, who decided to stop in Corrigan's saloon as he was on his way home. McCauley had never met Curly Bill, but after a couple of drinks at the establishment he was now part of the group. "I was on my way home when I stopped in Carrigan's [Corrigan's] saloon and met this party and we took a drink or two together, and some one proposed going up the street, and we all started out on the street," McCauley later recalled.[6] Once the party was on the street, one or more of the men "pulled their pistols and fired several shots."[7] According to McCauley, Curly Bill remarked, "This won't do, boys," but the shooting continued.[8] The promiscuous shooting at the "moon and stars on Allen street" created a commotion in the town and caused people to gather in the street.[9] Concerned that they might be arrested for the disturbance, Johnson, McCauley, and Curly Bill ran behind a building on the other side of the road.[10]

Town marshal Fred White suddenly appeared near the men behind the building, which was located in a vacant lot between Allen Street and Tough Nut Street, and he ordered Curly Bill to surrender his pistol.[11] At that moment, Deputy Sheriff Wyatt Earp, who had also responded to the shooting disturbance, arrived just in time to hear White say: "I am an officer; give me your pistol."[12] Upon White's command, Curly reached behind him and pulled his pistol out from the holster.[13] Suddenly, White grabbed the barrel of the pistol, and Earp, who was now directly behind the cowboy, wrapped his arms around Curly to see if he had any other weapons. "Now, you G-- d-- s-- of a b----, give up that pistol!" exclaimed Fred White, who "gave a quick jerk and the pistol went off."[14] Fred White yelled "I am shot" as he fell to the ground, "shot in the left groin."[15]

When the pistol discharged, Wyatt Earp hit Curly Bill in the head with his pistol, knocking him down. While Curly remained on the ground, Earp stepped over the cowboy and picked up the pistol, which had fallen from White's hands when the town marshal collapsed. After picking up the pistol, Wyatt grabbed Curly's collar and told him to get up. The cowboy immediately asked, "What have I done? I have not done anything to be arrested for."[16] His protest went unheard by Deputy Earp, and he was quickly placed in the city jail. Wyatt Earp, along with his brothers Virgil and Morgan, then went after the other men involved in the disturbance. The brothers succeeded in finding and arresting Ed Collins, Andrew Ames, Dick Lloyd, Frank Patterson, and James Johnson.[17] McCauley, however, had "skinned out and went home" after White was shot and managed to avoid being arrested by the deputy sheriff.[18] The next day the *Tombstone Epitaph* described the events leading up to the shooting of Marshal Fred White:

Shooting at Tombstone
[Tombstone Epitaph, October 28.]

About 12:30 last night a series of pistol shots startled the late goers on the streets, and visions of funerals, etc., flitted through the brain of the Epitaph local, and the result proved that his surmises were correct. The result in a few words is as follows: A lot of Texas cowboys, as they are called, began firing at the moon and stars on Allen street, near Sixth. City Marshal

White, who happened to be in the neighborhood, interfered to prevent violation of the city ordinance, and was ruthlessly shot by one of the number. Deputy Sheriff Earp, who is ever to the front when duty calls, arrived just in the nick of time. Seeing the Marshal fall, he promptly knocked his assailant down with a six shooter and as promptly locked him up; and with the assistance of his brothers Virgil and Morgan went in pursuit of the others. That he found them, an inventory of the City Prison this morning will testify. Marshal White was shot in the left groin, the ball passing nearly through, and being cut from the buttock by Dr. Matthews. The wound is a serious though not fatal one. Too much praise cannot be given to the Marshal for his gallant attempt to arrest the violators of the ordinance, nor to Deputy Sheriff Earp and his brothers for the energy displayed in bringing in the malefactors to arrest. At last accounts, 3 p.m., Marshal White was sleeping, and strong hopes of his ultimate recovery were expected.[19]

The following morning the Tombstone common council held a special meeting and appointed Virgil Earp temporary assistant marshal pending the "illness of Marshal White."[20] News of the shooting of town marshal Fred White quickly made its way to Tucson:

Fatal Shooting at Tombstone.
Special to the STAR
TOMBSTONE, Oct. 28.—A serious and perhaps fatal shooting affray occurred here last night, the victim of the deadly bullet being the City Marshal, Fred White. A company of five cow-boys who have been carousing about town for several days and boasting that if our officers interfered with them they would eat them, as they frequently dined on officers. About

midnight some of the party was going up Allen street and commenced firing off their pistols. Marshal White appeared on the scene and seized one of the cow-boys, who is known as Curley, and demanded his surrender. Curley resisted, and while the Marshal was struggling with him for the pistol, Deputy-Sheriff Earp and his brother arrived, but before they could disarm Curley he succeeded in discharging his pistol, the ball striking White in the groin and inflicting a serious if not fatal wound. Simultaneous with the shot Curley was knocked down by Earp and disarmed, and taken to the lock-up. Deputy Earp then started, with his two brothers, in pursuit of the rest of the gang, and soon returned four of them as prisoners.

Marshal White is in a very critical condition, and it is feared he cannot possibly recover. He was an efficient officer, and the community feels outraged that he was thus shot while in the discharge of his duty.

Curley waived examination this morning, and at noon officers started for Tucson, as there is fear of lynching him. This party of cow-boys are believed to be the same who committed the depredations at San Simon recently.[21]

The morning after the shooting, Curly was brought before Judge Michael Gray on a warrant made out by Wyatt Earp, charging him with assault with intent to murder. Curly Bill asked the court for a delay to secure counsel, which was granted. A short time later, at ten o'clock, Curly Bill appeared with his attorney, Judge John Haynes of Tucson, who had come to Tombstone to deliver a speech. The initial reports about White's condition were somewhat favorable; however, rumors began to circulate in town that Fred White would die by sundown. Fearing that a vigilance committee was forming to lynch him, Curly Bill, on advice of his counsel, chose to waive his examination before Gray, and he was quickly taken by Wyatt Earp and George Collins to Tucson for his own safety. The Tombstone newspapers continued to cover the story of Fred White's shooting and the arrest of the other men involved in the disturbance:

Assault to Murder

The party who shot Marshal White on Tuesday night was brought before Judge [Michael] Gray yesterday morning on a warrant charging him with assault to murder. The complaint was made by Deputy Sheriff Earp. The prisoner asked [for a delay until] 10 o'clock to enable him to secure counsel. At 10 o'clock the prisoner reappeared in company with his counsel, Judge [John] Haynes, of Tucson, and waiving examination, was committed to jail to await the next meeting of the Grand Jury. He gave the name William Rosciotis [Brocius] and claimed to hail from [the] San Simon country [about seventy five miles northeast of Tombstone, near the New Mexico line]. Rumor at the time being rife that Marshal White would not live until sundown, and that a Vigilance committee was organizing to hang the prisoner, it was deemed best to take him at once to Tucson. A buggy was at hand and Deputy Sheriff Earp, accompanied by George Collins, started. They were guarded for several miles out of town by Messrs. Virgil and Morgan Earp, and others.

Police Court

Edward Collins, A. Ames, R. Loyd, Frank Patterson and James Johnson were brought before Judge Gray yesterday morning on charge of violating city ordinances. A. Ames pleaded guilty to carrying concealed weapons and discharging same on the public streets. He was fined $40, which he paid.

Edward Collins, R. Loyd and James Johnson pleaded
guilty to carrying concealed weapons, and were fined
$10 each, which was paid. Frank Patterson was
discharged, it being made apparent to his Honor that
he had used every effort to prevent the disturbance
by his companions . . . .[22]

Curly Bill was transported to Tucson and placed in the Pima
County jail to await the disposition of his case. The Record of Prisoners
committed to the Pima County jail indicates that "William Brocious,"
was confined in the jail on October 28, 1880.[23] He was committed
by order of Judge Michael Gray of Tombstone and was charged with
"assault with a deadly weapon with intent to commit murder."[24] Two
days later, on October 30, Fred White died and he was buried the
next day. "The cortege following the murdered Marshal to the grave
was the largest ever seen in our embryo city. It embraced all classes
and conditions of society from the millionaire to the mudsill and
numbered fully 1,000 people," commented the *Tombstone Epitaph*.[25]
The day following White's funeral, the city council met and decided to
hold a special election on November 12 to fill the vacancy in the
marshal's office. Meanwhile, Virgil Earp remained acting city marshal
pending the special election. Ben Sippy beat out Virgil Earp in the
special election to become the new town marshal.

After taking Curly Bill to Tucson, Wyatt Earp and George
Collins stayed the night at the Palace Hotel before returning to
Tombstone. Upon his return to town, Earp told a reporter for the
Tombstone Epitaph that during the trip to Tucson Brocius had told
him that he was an escaped prisoner from Texas. The *Tombstone
Epitaph*, on October 31, 1880, wrote that Curly Bill was "an old
offender against the law," who had "stopped a stage in El Paso County,
Texas, killing one man and dangerously wounding another."[26]

At the time of the shooting of Fred White, few people in
Tombstone had ever heard of Curly Bill. Even fewer knew that the
cowboy was an escaped Texas felon or that he was believed to have
killed a man before coming to Arizona. Yet, the notoriety he received

in the Arizona newspapers following this fatal incident helped to bolster his reputation in the territory as a man-killer and notorious desperado. Thereafter, Curly Bill's infamy in Arizona grew rapidly by rumor and innuendo and with each newspaper article that was published about him. Nevertheless, no matter what outrage or crime the cowboy reportedly committed during the next year and a half, more than anything else, Curly Bill would always be best remembered as the man who shot Tombstone Marshal Fred White.[27]

5

TERRITORY OF ARIZONA VS. WILLIAM BROCIUS

Life in the Tucson jail was probably not too harsh on Curly Bill, who two years before had spent several months locked up in Texas.[1]   But there he sat, throughout November and most of December 1880, simply awaiting trial.[2] He had waived his hearing before Judge Gray because he feared that he might be lynched in Tombstone by a mob of citizens that were upset over the shooting of Fred White. Since his arrival in Tucson, the cowboy had been confined in the jail, with no hearing scheduled and no bond set.[3]

By December 1880, rumors began to reach Tucson that friends of "Curly the cowboy" wanted him freed or they would take matters into their own hands. On December 9, 1880, the *Arizona Daily Star* published the following article about the rumors being heard in town:

Needs Looking After
The rumor reaches us that the cowboy friends of Curly the cowboy who shot and killed Marshal White, at Tombstone, some time ago, say, in case he is tried and not acquitted they will come to Tucson in force and take him from jail. This may not be an idle threat, and no one acquainted with our jail will for a moment deny the ability of fifty or even twenty men to force an entrance, and in case such an event should occur there would be no one to blame but the Board of Supervisors.

They should have the windows secured with heavy
iron bars, a strong iron door at the front entrance,
and an iron grated door at the second, thus secured,
the jailors could hold 100 men at bay until
assistance arrived. Our jail is certainly anything
but secure, and should be attended to.

It is impossible to know which men in the San Simon Valley
were making the threats. However, Bob Martin, the man with
whom Curly Bill had escaped from the Texas Rangers in November
1878, likely would have helped his friend bust out of the Tucson
jail. Nevertheless, any possible attempt by Martin to free Brocius
was thwarted when Martin was killed by a gang of four rustlers in
late November 1880.[4] Still, Pony Deal, another Texas associate,
was in the area and probably would have assisted Curly Bill.
Likewise, San Simon cowboys Joe Hill and John Ringo, in Texas,
were known to free friends locked up in jail.[5]

Two years earlier, Curly Bill and Bob Martin had freed
themselves from the custody of the Texas Rangers using a file
secretly passed to them by a friend. A similar ploy was used in
Tucson by friends of the cowboy. Someone managed to smuggle
into the Tucson jail a thin-bladed knife for Curly Bill and a small
saw for another San Simon cowboy, William Shannon, alias Shorty,
who was charged with grand larceny. The cowboys' hopes of
freeing themselves from the jail were ended before they could
make good use of their "tools," though, when Deputy Sheriff
Buttner made a surprise search of the prisoners:

In the of the hat of Curly, the Texas cow boy, who
killed Marshal White at Tombstone, there was
found a small thin bladed knife, and under the coat
collar of the criminal Shannon, alias Shorty,
charged with grand larceny, was found a small saw,
such as criminals use for cutting iron bars, shackles,
&c. How or where they obtained those articles is

not known, but that they would have used them to possible good advantage no one doubts. The search was fortunate as well as commendable.[6]

Curly Bill's plan to break out of the Tucson jail may have been foiled by the surprise inspection, but it turned out to be a lucky break for the cowboy. J. C. Perry, his attorney, was working on an easier and far more legal way to free the cowboy. Eleven days after the reported search, on Monday, December 20, "William Brocius, better known under the nom de plume of Curly Bill," presented through his attorney, J. C. Perry, a verified petition to the court stating that the sheriff had held his client in jail for almost two months without any bail being set.[7] The petition argued that "he was arrested and placed in the lock up at Tombstone," and that because of the fear of mob violence, he waived his examination and was immediately taken to the county jail in Tucson for his own safety.[8] "[H]e was advised by counsel retained at the time for him, as well as the keepers and officers having him in charge, and acting upon their advice and under fear of such lynching he was taken before Justice Gray, where his counsel then waived examination, and he was thereupon forthwith transported from Tombstone to the county jail," wrote the *Arizona Daily Star*.[9]

The following day, on December 21, his attorney argued to Justice Joseph Neugass that the commitment of Curly Bill was defective because it did not "state any amount in which he [Brocius] could give bail." [10] Perry asked that his client be granted an examination before the court so that the evidence of what had occurred could exonerate him. In response, the district attorney, Hugh Farley, fought hard to prevent the hearing, arguing that the defendant had waived his examination and that he was no longer entitled to a hearing. Justice Neugass disagreed with the district attorney and allowed a hearing, which was scheduled for 2:00 p.m. on Wednesday, December 22, 1880.[11] The following day the *Arizona Weekly Star* reported that Curly Bill's hearing had commenced but was continued until December 24:

Examination
"The examination of Wm. Brocius, -"Curly Bill"-
For the shooting of the late marshal Fred White,
at Tombstone, was commenced yesterday before
Justice Nuegass and continued until tomorrow to
allow the defense to obtain important witnesses."[12]

On Friday, December 24, the day before Christmas, the
necessary witnesses were not present and the hearing was again
postponed:

Postponed.
"The examination of "Curly Bill," before Judge
Neugass, was postponed again yesterday until
Monday afternoon. The non-presence of some
important witnesses caused the recent
postponement." [13]

Two days after Christmas, on December 27, 1880, the
examination was held before Justice Neugass. Several witnesses
came forward to exonerate Curly Bill of acting criminally in the
death of Marshal Fred White. The *Citizen* published the testimony
given before Neugass, as well as a brief summary of his decision
in the case:

"Curly Bill"
His Examination Concluded Before Justice
Neugass - Important Testimony For The Defense
The Justice's Decision.

The examination of William Brocious [Brocius]
alias Curly Bill, charged with murder in the killing
of Marshal White, of Tombstone, was concluded
this morning before Justice of the Peace Neugass.
All the testimony is clear and decidedly to the point.

Wyatt S. Earp, was called for the territory, testified: On the 27th of last October was Deputy Sheriff; resided at Tombstone; saw defendant that night at the time Marshal White was shot; was present at the time the fatal shot fired; saw Mr. Johnson there at that time; my brother came up immediately after; this affair occurred back of a building in a vacant lot between Allen and Tough Nut streets; I was in Billy Owen's saloon and heard three or four shots fired; upon hearing the first shot I ran out in the street and I saw the flash of a pistol up the street about a block from where I was; several shots were fired in quick succession; ran up as quick as I could, and when I got there I met my brother, Morgan Earp, and a man by the name of [Fred] Dodge; I asked my brother who it was that did the shooting; he said he didn't know—some fellows who run behind that building; I asked him for his six shooter and he sent me to Dodge; after I got the pistol, I run around the building, and as I turned the corner I ran past this man Johnson, who was standing near the corner of the building; I ran between him and the corner of the building; but before I got there I heard White say: "I am an officer; give me your pistol;" and just as I was almost there I saw the defendant pull his pistol out of his scabbard and Marshal White grabbed hold of the barrel of it; the parties were not more than two feet apart facing each other; both had hold of the pistol, and just then I threw my arms around the defendant, to see if he had any other weapons, and looked over his shoulder, and White saw me and said: "Now, you G— d— s— of a b— give up that pistol;" and he gave a quick jerk and the pistol went off; White had it in his hands, and when he fell to the ground, shot, the pistol dropped and I picked it up; as he fell, he said, "I am shot." The defendant stood still from the time I first saw him until the pistol went off; when I took defendant in charge he said, "what have I done? I have not done anything to be arrested for." When the pistol exploded I knocked defendant down with my six-shooter; he did not get up until I stepped over and picked up the pistol, which had fallen out of White's hands as he fell. I then walked up to defendant, caught him by the collar and told him to get up. I did not notice that he was drunk; if he was I did not notice it. When I turned the corner he was in the act of taking his pistol out of his scabbard. I examined the pistol afterwards and found only one cartridge discharged, five remaining. The pistol was a Colt's 45 calibre.

James K. Johnson, called for the Territory, testified as follows: I live in Charleston [a mill town ten miles southwest of Tombstone]; have lived there about four months; am a miner; know defendant. The evening of the occurrence I was with Mr. Brocius and several others. Some one proposed going up the street, and as we got in the street some one pulled a pistol and fired. Brocius said "don't do that," but they fired several more shots, and defendant and I ran across the street. There was a terrible rush of people and Marshal White came up and demanded defendant's pistol; said he was an officer [and] for him to give up his gun. I was standing about ten feet away, and just then Wyatt Earp ran past me, between me and the corner of the building, and as defendant was giving up the pistol, white jerked hold of it and said, " You d-d son of a b-h; give up that gun," and then the pistol went off; I am positive that Defendant did not have the pistol in his hands until White demanded it and then pulled it from his scabbard; defendant, McCauley and myself ran behind this building to keep away from the crowd; we were afraid we would be arrested and ran behind to get out of the way.

Andrew McCauley - called for Territory, sworn, testified as follows: Live in Tombstone; have lived there two years; never met defendant till the night of this shooting occurrence; I was on my way home when I stopped in Carrigan's [Thomas Corrigan's] saloon and met this party and we took a drink or two together, and some one proposed going up the street, and we started out on the street; as we were going along some of the boys pulled their pistols and fired several shots; I said to Johnson, "let's get out of this," and we ran across the street; I heard defendant make the remark, "this won't do, boys" just before we started across the street; we had just stopped behind this building when marshal White made his appearance; I do not know which direction he came from or whether he was standing there when we arrived; anyway, he said he was an oficer, and demanded defendant's pistol; I was about 10 or 15 feet away; the defendant put his hand behind him and commenced pulling his pistol, and when it got out enough so White could, he grabbed hold of it and just then Earp ran up and took hold of defendant and White said, "Now, then, you G— d— s— of a b—, give that up, and jerked it and it went off; and I skinned out and went home.

Dr. H. M. [Henry Matthews], called for Territory,
testified as follows: I am a practicing physician;
reside at Tombstone; attended deceased White
before he died; his death was occasioned by
peritonitis, caused by the gun-shot wound; from
the looks of the wound, the pistol was held at an
angle of about 45 degrees.

Jacob Gruber testified: I am a gunsmith; have
examined the pistol in evidence; find a defect in it
in this, that the pistol can be discharged at half-
cock.

Morgan Earp testified substantially to the same
effect as Wyatt Earp, and the statement of
defendant Brocious coincided in every respect with
the testimony for the territory.

Judge Neugass, in a lengthy review of the case,
discharged the prisoner from custody, the testimony
showing clearly that he was not warranted in
binding him over.[14]

Curly Bill's murder hearing had generated a great deal of
interest from the public and in the press, and the *Arizona Daily
Star,* on December 28, 1878, decided to published Justice Neugass'
full decision:

The White Tragedy.
As this case has attracted much attention and has
been the subject of considerable comment, both in
our city and Tombstone, we publish the decision
in full, as rendered by Justice Neugass yesterday
afternoon, discharging the prisoner:

Wyatt Earp's testimony before Justice Neugass helped Curly Bill Brocius get a dismissal of the murder charge for killing Fred White.

Territory of Arizona vs. William Brocius. Decision.

The defendant in the above entitled proceedings having by his counsel, J. C. Perry, Esq., on December 20th, 1880, filed in this court, a duly verified petition from which it appearing that the petitioner was charged with assault with intent to kill, upon the person of one Frederick White, and that he had been committed to the county jail without bail by M. Gray, Esq., Justice of the Peace of Precinct No. 17, that such assault had occurred at a time of great public excitement, immediately prior to the general election, in November last, that threats of lynching said petitioner were freely made at the time, and that acting under the advice and under fear of mob violence the petitioner waived examination and was immediately committed without bail.

Upon this petition, argument was duly heard by defendant's counsel, and the District Attorney, Hugh Farley, Esq., and at its conclusion an examination was ordered by me for the following reasons:

The statute provides that after the witnesses for the Territory shall have been examined the defendant may waive his right to make a statement in relation to the charge against him, that it does not provide for, nor contemplate a total waiver of any examination whatever into the charge against him in the first instance. An inquiry to some extent at least would seem to be required for purposes of public justice. It may be that a commitment and a bond would constitute a bar to any other or further examination into the charge by another magistrate upon proper application to him for that purpose.

It would seem indeed that in dealing with the higher grade of felonies at least, the judicial conscience of the magistrate holding the inquiry ought, in some legal way, to be informed of the circumstances attending the commission of the alleged crimes before he could properly determine what amount of bail would probably secure the attendance of the accused to answer the charges, which is the object to be attained by the preliminary examination. Of course, no blame, using the language of C. Justice Wallace, in ex parte Walsh, 39 Cal., can be imputed to the Justices of the Peace acting in this instance. For in proceeding upon the waiver of the accused he only pursued a course of practice which has become somewhat general in this Territory, but it is a practice which I think is not authorized by statute, and ought not to be encouraged, for it is liable to abuse, and where that course is adopted it should not be held to preclude a second or further examination, when such further or second examination is properly insitituted and conducted according to the statutory reguirements. Such examination having therefore been accorded to the defendant herein, has been duly proceeded with and held upon the 22nd, 24th, and 27th days of December instant, and upon which the following facts have been adduced in evidence,

It appears from the evidence that the defendant, on the night of Oct. 27th, was at Tombstone and in company with some of his friends and some strangers to him, was standing in one of the public streets of Tombstone about the hour of midnight. That some of the party were under the influence of liquor, and that they commenced shooting pistols off in the air, whereupon the defendant, with two of his companions, to avoid arrest, ran across the street and behind a building upon the opposite side, the rest of the party went in another direction. Almost immediately after their arrival behind the building, the deceased, F. White came up to defendant, told him he was an officer and demanded his pistol, at the same time that the defendant was drawing and handing his pistol to White, Wyatt Earp, a deputy sheriff, ran behind the defendant and threw his arms around him. White, who recognized Earp, then grabbed the pistol with both hands around the barrel, and using an opprobrious epithet, tore the pistol with great force from the hands of defendant, and in so doing exploded it and the ball entered White's body. Sheriff Earp at once knocked down defendant, arrested and locked him up. At the time the defendant protested his innocence, and it appears in evidence that he was unacquainted with White, and that there was no enmity or hard feeling in any way between the two men. Earp testifies that he considers the shooting of White as accidental, and he is corroborated in all his statements by the testimony of two other witnesses present— McCauley and Johnson, **and by the declaration or dying statement of the deceased under oath.**

It appears also that the pistol which the defendant had, and which caused the death of White, is defective in its workings, and that it was in such condition as to be easily exploded. Only one cartridge had been exploded, showing that defendant had not fired any of the prior shots and tending to corroborate his statement that he was in the act of voluntarily surrendering it when White tore it from his hand.

It appears, therefore, to my satisfaction, from all the evidence adduced before me, that the defendant was not doing any unlawful act at the time of the unfortunate shooting and that he had not, prior thereto, committed any breach of the peace, but to the contrary thereof was in the act of going away to avoid any difficulty or trouble.

Now, homicide, or the killing of any human creature is of three kinds, justifiable, excusable and by misadventure and felonious. The first has no share of guilt at all, the second very little, the third is the very highest crime against the law of nature that a man is capable of committing.

All the evidence adduced before me tends clearly to placing the killing in the second class of homicide by misadventure. The defendant was engaged in no unlawful acts; was complying with the demand of an official of the law in a peaceable and lawful way; was surrendering his weapon as demanded, when the deceased forcibly and without any necessity therefor tore the pistol from his hand, exploding it in so doing and inflicted by that act the wound upon himself from which he died.

Upon the foregoing facts and upon the fully corroborated statement of the accused and believing the defendant to be guiltless of any intention to hurt or injure the deceased and that such killing was by misadventure and excusable in law, I order the defendant to be discharged from custody. [Emphasis added].

Testimony was also heard that White had made a deathbed statement to the effect that the shooting was not intentional. Justice Neugass called the killing a "homicide by misadventure," and the court dismissed the charge against Curly Bill.

Despite the court's decision that Curly Bill's killing of Fred White was an accident, many people continued to believe that Curly Bill Brocius had intentionally killed Fred White. Some even suggested that Curly Bill had used a pistol trick popularly called the "border roll," where a man holds the pistol with its butt end toward another man, deceptively feigning the surrender of his weapon, only to suddenly roll the gun into firing position at the last second. About the trick, the *Silver City Enterprise* later noted: "Curley Bill could do it the best of the lot, and that's how he killed Sheriff White at Tombstone."[15] Deputy Sheriff William Breakenridge later recalled Curly showing him the trick: "He told me never to let a man give his pistol butt end toward me, and showed me why. He handed me his gun that way, and as I reached to take it he whirled it on his finger, and it was cocked, staring me in the face, and ready to shoot. His advice was, that if I disarmed anyone to make him throw his pistol down."[16] It's doubtful that Curly Bill had used the pistol trick when he shot Tombstone's town marshal. Under the fast-moving circumstances, the ploy would have required a tremendous amount of skill to accomplish successfully without being noticed by anyone, including Fred White and Wyatt Earp. Most likely, the shooting was really an accident, but Curly Bill allowed people to assume, for the reputation that it brought him, that he had intentionally killed White.

While Curly Bill was incarcerated in the Tucson jail, the Pima County election was held. The results created a great deal of controversy. The vote counts in San Simon, Tombstone, and other places in the southeastern portion of Pima County were questioned for discrepancies. It seems that more people voted than were registered in some of these locations. At Precinct 27, for San Simon Cienega, the polling place was to be at Joe Hill's house, and election officials for the precinct included Ike Clanton, John Ringo, and A. H. Thompson.[17] The Pima County Board of Supervisors had doubts over the residency of the board election officials and the location of the polling place. Later it revoked its previous order appointing Clanton, Ringo, and Thompson. It then appointed two different men as polling officials and changed the location of the vote.[18] The overall election results were close, giving Charles Shibell a narrow victory over Bob Paul for Pima County sheriff. Paul contested the results and eventually was named Pima County sheriff after a court battle.[19] Wyatt Earp later claimed, categorically and without corroboration, that he had helped Paul in some way to uncover information about the voting irregularities.[20]

The San Simon election fraud became part of Tombstone folklore, and old-timers often repeated stories about how the cowboys of San Simon, including Curly Bill, took "charge of" the poll.[21] Nevertheless, at the time of the election, Curly Bill was in the Pima County jail in Tucson, over a hundred miles away.[22]

Bob Paul almost lost his bid to win the postion of Pima County
Sheriff in the November 1880 election due to the vote at San
Simon. Tombstone folklore often portrays Curly Bill as a main
culprit in the rigged vote. But, in actuality, the notorious cowboy
was locked up in the Pima County jail at the time of the election.

6

COME AND GET ME

To mark the first stage of his transformation from a rowdy
Texas desperado to a notorious Arizona outlaw gang leader, Curly
Bill celebrated his release and the New Year by "treeing" Charleston
and Contention City. The White killing and the newspaper reports
that covered the story had made him a notorious individual in the
territory. It appears that he reveled in this reputation and that he acted
with much more bravado following his release. He would, in a short
time, be considered the most notorious outlaw in the territory.

Around January 9, 1881, Curly Bill and a few others arrived
at Charleston, a mill town near the San Pedro River about 10 miles
southwest of Tombstone, and generally proceeded to torment the
inhabitants of the town. The next day stories of what happened at
Charleston made their way to Tombstone and to George Parsons
who noted the incident in his diary:

> Monday, [January] 10th [1881]: Some more bullying
> by the Cow boys. 'Curly Bill' & others captured
> Charleston the other night & played the devil generally
> breaking up a religious meeting by chasing the minister
> out of the house putting out lights with pistol balls &
> going through the town.[1]

Reports of the "treeing" of Charleston by Curly Bill also quickly
traveled to Tucson, and the *Arizona Weekly Star* informed Tucson of
the cowboy's latest escapade: "Last Sunday, a week ago, Curly Bill,
with a lot of cowboys, took in a church four miles from Charleston.
While the services were proceeding the gang went in and Curly Bill

cooly told the parson to stop his talk, or he would shoot an eye out."[2]

Nine days later, the notorious cowboy's next stop was the town of Contention City, where he and a group of men began to quickly wreak havoc on the south end of the town. Later that afternoon the cowboys moved their operations to the north side of town, where they committed grave outrages like "shooting at a peaceable citizen, of robbing a till of $50, and other offenses equally unpardonable."[3] Around eight o'clock that evening citizens went before the justice of the peace to file complaints regarding the outrages. In response to the numerous filed complaints, the justice prepared and issued warrants for the rowdy cowboys' arrest. But when Deputy T. B. Ludwig tried to make an arrest on the cowboys, Curly Bill and a companion named George resisted by "drawing their Henry rifles."[4] Following Ludwig's ineffectual effort to arrest the men, some citizens gathered in the street later that evening, intent on standing up to the cowboys; however, the desperadoes paid little attention to the citizens' attempt at restoring law and order in the small mining town. As the opposing groups faced each other, gunfire erupted on both sides, but nobody was injured in the battle. The cowboys, having succeeded in causing a ruckus in Contention City for the better part of a full day, eventually rode out of town looking for new adventures.

After leaving Contention City, Curly Bill stayed for two days at nearby Waterville, and no effort to arrest him was made by any officer, despite the complaints against him filed with the justice of the peace at Contention City. Even more surprising, Curly Bill reportedly dared the county authorities to come and get him, but the challenge was not accepted. "This bravado sent messages to some of the deputy sheriffs that he was there and to come and take him," noted the *Arizona Daily Star*.[5] According to one newspaper report, at the time of the challenge, Curly Bill was seen wearing "two belts of cartridges, a revolver, and a Henry rifle."[6] About Curly Bill's latest spree, the *Arizona Daily Star* commented: "It is an enigma to most of our people why these outlaws, and others of their kind, are not arrested by the county officers."[7] The newspaper declared that it was time for the community to stand up to men such as these:

The time has come to make this community too hot to
hold them. The terror these men have caused the
traveling public, as well as the residents along the San
Pedro, is having a serious influence, and this scab on
the body politic, needs a fearless operation to remove
it. Let the Sheriff and his deputies see to it.[8]

The *Arizona Daily Star*, noting that the sheriff and his deputy
had the authority and ability to call out a sufficient number of men to
take in these evildoers, concluded: "It is no trouble to find the rascals,
for they are not hiding, and defy the laws."[9]

Criticism proliferated on the news that Curly Bill, the cowboy
who had killed Marshal Fred White in Tombstone, was now causing
more problems in southeastern Arizona since his release from jail.
Tucson began receiving dispatches from Tombstone that openly voiced
the town's disappointment with Neugass' decision that Curly Bill
Brocius had not intentionally killed Fred White. Weary of the criticism
from Tombstone, the *Arizona Weekly Citizen*, on January 22, 1881,
made the following suggestion for the people of the soon-to-be-formed
Cochise County:

A Suggestion
The Epitaph rages on the subject of Curly Bill, and is
not satisfied with the disposal of the case when he
was exaimined on the charge of killing Marshal Fred
White. Now we make a suggestion. The death of
White occurred in what will be a part of the new
county of Cachise. [sic]

Curly Bill has never been tried for the homicide and
is subject to arrest upon the charge of murder any
day. He can be found at any time within the limits of
Cachise [sic] county. Let the Epitaph man securc his
indictment by the First Grand Jury that meets in the
new county, and see what a jury over there will do. It

will be a good case for the new District Attorney to commence upon.

On February 1, 1881, the Arizona legislature created Cochise County by shearing off a large chunk of eastern Pima County.[10] Crimes previously committed in the new county were now within the jurisdiction of that county's prosecutor's office.[11] While no further effort was apparently made by Cochise County officials against Curly Bill for the White killing, it appears that a different complaint against the cowboy captioned "Territory vs. Curly Bill" was filed in Cochise County.[12] Unfortunately, the crime that was the basis of the complaint is not known, and in May 1881 the grand jury failed to indict Brocius that term.

Over a year later, Curly Bill received national attention based on the events that occurred in January 1881, when *The National Police Gazette* published an article based on information provided by James Hume, the Chief of Detectives for Wells, Fargo:

> 'Curly Bill' . . . is viewed with terror in Cochise County. His escapades and outrages have been numberless. There is nothing he dare not do and everyone is afraid of him . . . One night about a year ago, finding Tombstone an unpleasant residence in consequence of a murder he had committed there (he was acquitted by a jury packed with cowboys) he went to Charleston, a short distance from that town. It was night when he and a pal arrived and a Mexican fandango was in progress. They entered the ball room and each placed his back against the door at either end of the apartment. They then drew their pistols. Stop! cried he. Everyone knew the desperate character of the men and stopped as commanded. Strip, everyone of you! shouted Bill. They did so without hesitation. Strike up the music; now then, dance. And men and women in a state of perfect nudity

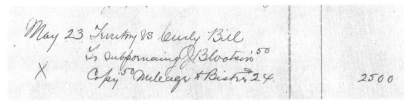

Sheriff John Behan sent a deputy to Bisbee to serve a subpoena on a man, who was to testify before the grand jury in a case against Curly Bill Brocius. Cochise County Records, MS 180, Box 11, Arizona Historical Society Library, Tucson, Arizona.

were made to dance madly for an hour at the point of
the desperado's pistol.[13]

While the cowboy's hell raising at the religious meeting was
mentioned by the *Arizona Weekly Star* and by George Parsons in his
diary, Hume's story of the nude dancing was not published at the time
in the newspapers. It is not known whether his retelling of the story
mirrors the actual event. Nevertheless, the description of Curly Bill
presented by Hume in a national newspaper gave Brocius far-reaching
recognition. He had made the transformation from an ordinary Texas
bad man to a notorious Arizona desperado and cowboy gang leader.
On one occasion, Tom Thornton, a hotel keeper from
Galeyville who was visiting San Francisco, was asked by a reporter,
"How is it that this Curly Bill has acquired such a name as a desperado
in Arizona?" [14] Thornton replied, "Oh, just because you paper men
chose to give it to him." [15] Thornton then recalled:

> The worst trick I ever knew him to do was to go into
> a restuarant once, while the people were at dinner.
> He was drunk and pulled out his two revolvers and
> laid them beside his plate, and ordered every one at
> the table to wait until he was through, as it was
> ungentlemanly and impolite to rise before all had
> finished their meal. Of course, everybody in the
> restaurant sat and waited until Bill got done eating,
> but he was so full he laid down his head upon his
> arms and fell asleep, and the folks were so afraid of
> him that that they supposed he was just shamming
> sleep as to get a chance to shoot the first one who
> rose from the table. They all waited until he awoke,
> when he paid the bill for the crowd and left.[16]

Most of Curly Bill's rowdy and raucous behavior in the outer
communities and small settlements of Arizona never made the
newspapers at the time the acts were committed. Nevertheless, some

recollections of the cowboy's antics have survived. For example, the *New Southwest and Grant County Herald*, on April 8, 1882, wrote the following about Curly Bill: "His playful exhibition of his skill with the pistol never failed to delight those communities which the pirepatetic William favored with his presence. Lieut. Mahoney, a well-known journalist of this city, still carefully preserves a hat with a bullet-hole of Bill's making. Bill objected to the style of the article, and signified his disgust by shooting a ball through it." The *Silver City Enterprise*, on November 23, 1883, noted another incident involving Curly Bill:

> Curly Bill whipped out his revolver and for amusement shot a hole through the top of a frieghter's hat. . . . A few minutes afterwards a cry of fire was raised, and the gin mill where Curly Bill and his companions were soon burned to the ground. . . . Curly Bill got to shooting at a lamp and hit too low, and it exploded. He will pay for the damages though.

Of course, there is no way to substantiate or refute the above stories of Curly Bill's hell raising pranks in Silver City and other towns. However, the *Arizona Weekly Citizen*, on May 14, 1882, generally noted that "cowboys have broken whiskey glasses just as they were raised to the lips by terror stricken citizens, broken the tops of beer bottles and snuffed out candles with their revolvers." Therefore, Curly Bill likely participated in this type of activity when "treeing" a town.

During 1881, rumors of cowboy depredations in the area began to be reported more frequently in the newspapers. However, the men who were responsible for the crimes usually were not personally identified. Instead, newspapers loosely described them as cowboys:

OUTLAWS
The depredations of the cow boys are becoming as frequent and of such magnitude that no time should be left in adopting measures which will insure either

their total extermination, or their departure from the
Territory. Not less than two hundred of these
marauding thieves infest the southeast section of
Arizona. . . . These bands of thieves go armed to the
teeth and show up in all directions, take in small
settlements and cause terror wherever they make their
appearance. [17]

The term "cowboy" was used indiscriminately by newspapers
and the public as a means of labeling the often unidentified outlaws
committing crimes in Arizona and Mexico. "'Cow-boys' is a generic
designation, originally applied to Cow drivers and herders in Western
Texas, but the name has been corrupted in the Territories of New
Mexico and Arizona and its local significance includes the lawless
element that exists upon the border, who subsist by rapine plunder
and highway robbery, and whose amusements are drunken orgies,
and murder," noted E. B. Pomroy, the United States Attorney for
Arizona.[18]

Tombstone folklore often portrays the cowboys of Arizona
as one organized gang, whose mission was to wreak havoc and commit
crimes in both the United States and Mexico. Nevertheless, while
cowboys congregated in the same places, drank and caroused in the
same saloons, and even freely associated with one another at times,
only rumor and innuendo suggest that these men were part of a single
gang. In actuality, there were several factions of men commonly
described as cowboys that may have associated with one another
while at towns like Galeyville and San Simon, but they owed no special
allegiance to any one man or gang. Instead, each faction had a small
core of men that generally rode together. It appears that some men
did occasionally ride with different groups. Curly Bill's so-called gang
included men like Billy Grounds, Zwing Hunt, Led Moore, and Jim
Hughes.[19] Some of the others that probably rode at one time or
another with Brocius in Arizona were: Bob Martin, Jim Wallace, Dick
Lloyd, Sandy King, Russian Bill, Pony Diehl, and Milt and Will Hicks.[20]

Many of the cowboys were rowdy and troublesome and often wreaked havoc in the smaller, remote communities in Cochise County. A letter published by the *Arizona Daily Star* on February 17, 1881, describes some of the hell-raising activities that occurred in these outlying areas:

> Of late, the little City of Maxey, which is situated on the Gila river near Camp Thomas, has on several occasions, been thrown into a high state of excitement by a party of men who syle themselves as Texas Cowboys, by riding through the place at a breakneck speed, and shooting off their pistols in the air, endangering the peaceful lives of the inhabitants, making it unsafe for anyone to venture on the street. They have gone so far as to ride into the stores and saloons. . . .

On March 8, Dick Lloyd, who was one of the cowboys arrested with Curly Bill in Tombstone the night Fred White was shot, rode into the camp. "He was in the habit of coming to Fort Thomas every few months and getting rip roaring drunk. After a few drinks he would get on his horse and with a Texas cowboy's 'Whoop-ee!' dash through the streets on a run firing his pistol into the air," according to William Breakenridge.[21] He was considered quarrelsome when drinking. Melvin Jones claimed that Dick Lloyd was a friend of Curly Bill and that the two men had come to Arizona together on the same cattle drive.[22]

Dick Lloyd entered O'Neil's saloon where Curly Bill, John Ringo, Joe Hill, and the other cowboys were playing cards. He then left the bar because some of the men did not like him. He went over to Mann's saloon, where he quickly got into an argument with Mann, the proprietor, and shot him. Lloyd seriously wounded Mann, but he survived. The cowboy ran back toward O'Neil's saloon and stole a horse belonging to Joe Hill. Before he left town, a wild idea came to him, and he rode straight into O'Neil's saloon, shooting and yelling.

According to some old-timers, that was Dick Lloyd's last ride—John Ringo, Joe Hill, Curly Bill, and the rest of the men shot and killed him.[23] Afterwards, according to the account, Jack O'Neil claimed that he alone had shot Dick Lloyd. The *Arizona Weekly Star* confirmed that O'Neil took responsibility for the killing:

A Dead Cow-Boy

Maxey, March 8. - Dick Loyed [sic], a cow-boy shot E. Mann this evening. After the shooting he rode into Oneil [sic] & Franklin's Saloon, where some person shot him dead. Oneil [sic] gave himself up as the party who shot him. We have no Justice to act as coroner. I summoned seven persons to investigate the case. It was justifiable. Mann will survive. Will abide instructions.

Collins [24]

Other than old-timers' recollections, there is no proof that Curly Bill and the other poker players shot the rambunctious cowboy. Officially, O'Neil claimed responsibility for the killing of Dick Lloyd. Nevertheless, the story of the shooting of Dick Lloyd by the cowboys at Maxey has become part of Tombstone folklore.

7

THE DEPUTY ASSESSOR

The San Simon Valley provided the perfect rural environment that allowed Curly Bill to roam around without much concern about running into territorial law officers. Still, deputies from Tombstone did occasionally venture out to the remote sections of Cochise County. In April 1881, Deputy Sheriff William M. Breakenridge, who had been appointed to this position earlier in the month by Sheriff John Behan, traveled to the railhead town of San Simon to serve a summons on a merchant.[1] Years later, Breakenridge recalled his trip to San Simon and the first time he met Curly Bill.

Rather than riding the long distance by horse, the deputy had taken the train to the railhead community. After serving the summons on the merchant, he was left to await the arrival of the next train for his return trip. He walked down the street and entered a saloon operated by a man named Shorty. The deputy noticed that there were several cowboys playing cards. In another area of the saloon, he saw a man lying on a card table. Though he did not know who the cowboy was at the time, he later learned that he was the notorious Curly Bill Brocius, the man who had shot Fred White. According to Breakenridge, "he was fully six feet tall, with black curly hair, freckled face, and well built."[2]

A short time later the saloon keeper came into the room with a bucket of water and began to take a drink with a tin cup. Curly Bill immediately raised up on his elbow and shot the cup out of his hand. Brocius quickly explained that the cup contained urine—not water. Afterwards, it was discovered that the bullet had passed through the wall of the saloon and had killed Curly Bill's horse.[3]

John Behan, Cochise County's first sheriff, appointed William M. Breakenridge as a deputy sheriff on April 6, 1881.

Some time after this encounter, probably around the first week of May 1881, Breakenridge was given the task by Sheriff Behan to collect taxes in Cochise County, which had only recently been formed on February 1, 1881.[4] This was the first time anyone had tried to gather taxes in the southeastern portion of the territory. After collecting taxes in the Sulphur Springs valley and Willcox, the deputy spent the night at Prue's ranch. The following day he headed toward Galeyville, "where no taxes had ever been collected, and where rustlers held full sway."[5] Breakenridge later claimed that he had conceived of a plan to ask Curly for assistance in collecting the taxes in the area. Upon his arrival in Galeyville, he approached George Turner, whom he described as the cowboys' banker, and he asked to meet Curly Bill. The two men walked over to Babcock's saloon, and Turner called for Brocius to come out. Turner then introduced Curly Bill to the deputy sheriff. "I told him who I was and what I was, and said I wanted to hire him to go with me as a deputy assessor and help me collect taxes, as I was afraid I might be held up and my tax money taken from me if I went alone," Breakenridge later wrote.[6] "The idea of my asking the chief of all the cattle rustlers in that part of the country to help me collect taxes from them struck him as a good joke."[7] After thinking about the deputy's offer for a moment, Curly Bill laughed and agreed to help him. Breakenridge later fondly recalled his trip into the country to collect taxes with the notorious cowboy:

> Next day we started and he led me into a lot of blind canons [sic] and hiding-places where the rustlers had a lot of stolen Mexican cattle, and introduced me something like this:
> 'Boys, this is the county assessor, and I am his deputy. We are all good, law-abiding citizens here, and we cannot run the county without we pay our taxes.'
> He knew about how many cattle they each had, and if they demurred, or claimed they had no money, he made them give me an order on their banker

Turner. Curly had many a hearty laugh about it. He told them that if any of them should get arrested, it would be a good thing to show that they were taxpayers in the county.

I was treated fine by all of them, and I never want to travel with a better companion than Curly was on that trip. He was a remarkable shot with a pistol, and would hit a rabbit every time when it was running thirty or forty yards away. He whirled his pistol on his forefinger, and cocked it as it came up. . . . I learned one thing with him, and that was that he would not lie to me. What he told me he believed, and his word to me was better than the oaths of some of whom were known as good citizens.[8]

The deputy safely returned to Tombstone with nearly three thousand dollars from his county tour collecting taxes with Curly Bill. The *Tombstone Epitaph* on May 8, 1881, noted: "Sheriff Behan is making good progress in his assessment of the county. He thinks the roll when completed will foot up two million dollars." Of course, the thought of Curly Bill, "Arizona's Most Famous Outlaw," being deputized to help collect taxes might have created some strange discussions in Tombstone. A week later, on May 15, 1881, the *Tombstone Epitaph*, possibly referring to the tax collection method, commented: "Our Representatives by the grace of the San Simon cow-boys are happy."

There is no way to confirm Breakenridge's claim that Curly Bill was a remarkable shot, but there are accounts of the cowboy's shooting abilities:

He went up to Shakespeare once and filled up with rot-gut, and then commenced to show off his shootin'. He knocked the spot out o' the ace o' hearts and put three bullets in the same hole, and then had his pard Jake Wallace, to stand some twenty feet an' let him

Deputy sheriff William Breakenridge asked Curly
Bill to help him collect taxes in the southeastern
portion of Cochise County.

knock off a half dollar from between Jake's thumb and forefinger. And he did it every time. There was a soldier from Fort Bowie standing looking on, and Curley asked him if he would hold up the coin. The blame fool consented, and sure enough Bill knocked the coin from between his fingers, and asked him to hold it again. He held it up with his right hand and the next time Bill shot off his thumb, cooly remarking, as he put up his six-shooter, "Guess I've given ye yer discharge in full."[9]

There is no way to prove or refute the colorful story of Curly Bill's pistol-coin trick, but one can't help be skeptical about the account. Still, more than one newspaper article repeated the claim of Curly Bill shooting a soldier's finger off.[10]

8

THE NOTED DESPERADO SHOT

Following his excursion through the countryside helping Deputy Breakenridge collect taxes for the county, Curly Bill returned to Galeyville. On Thursday, May 19, Curly Bill was drinking in a saloon with several other cowboys when Breakenridge happened along. The deputy had come to Galeyville after conducting official business at San Simon.[1] Jim Wallace, one of Curly Bill's "partners and fast friends for the past five or six months," rode into town on a fine sorrel horse and joined Curly Bill's group playing cards and drinking.[2] "A constable named Goodman, who lived there, came past and noticed the fine horse and asked Wallace where he got it," Breakenridge recalled.[3] Somewhat insulted by the question, Wallace pulled his pistol and shot at the ground near the constable's heels. The officer fled the area as fast as possible. Wallace later made an insulting remark to Breakenridge, who simply turned and walked away.

Shortly after this incident, Curly Bill wanted Wallace to apologize to Breakenridge, his former tax collecting companion, and made the cowboy go find the deputy. "Curly, who was about half drunk, took Wallace to task for trying to pick a fuss with the officers, and every time he looked out the door and saw the horse with the white face he threatened to shoot it, but the others talked him out of it."[4] According to Breakenridge, Wallace "told me that Curly was very angry with him, and told him he had to apologize to me."[5] Wallace asked him to go to the saloon with him. At the saloon, Wallace apologized to Breakenridge, who thought everything was all right, "but, Curly, who was still drinking, wanted to have a row with Wallace and still threatened to shoot the horse."[6]

Curly Bill walked across the street to Babcock's saloon, where
he was joined by Wallace, and the two men exchanged some words.
"Curly told him to keep away and not to bother him any more or he
would shoot him as well as the horse," wrote Breakenridge.[7] Wallace
left Babcock's saloon, and a few moments later Curly came out of the
saloon, stepped off the porch, and began to get on his horse. Suddenly,
Wallace came up from behind Curly Bill and shot him on the left side
of the neck, the ball passing out through the cowboy's right cheek.
Curly Bill fell to the ground, seriously wounded, and Wallace was
seized by several cowboys who wanted to lynch him. Breakenridge
took him into custody, however, and brought him before Justice
Ellenwood, who later discharged him upon evidence that he had acted
in self-defense. Early reports of the shooting incident reached Tucson,
and on May 22, 1881, the *Arizona Citizen* pronounced Curly Bill
dead:

> Curley Bill Killed.
> Curley Bill, a notorious outlaw, was shot and instantly
> killed at Galeyville Thursday afternoon by his partner,
> Jim Wallace. They had both been drinking, and had
> a few hot words several times during the day. Finally,
> Curley Bill threatened to shoot Wallace 'on general
> principles,' but the latter slipped out the door and
> waited until Bill appeared, and shot him. Wallace
> was arrested by Deputy Sheriff Breakenridge and
> taken before Justice Ellenwood, who discharged the
> prisoner upon evidence that he committed the deed
> in self defense. Immediately, upon being set free,
> Wallace left on horseback for parts unknown.

Four days later, on May 26, 1881, the *Tombstone Nugget*
clarified, much to the regret of many residents, that the early report of
the notorious cowboy's sudden demise was grossly exaggerated and
that Arizona's most famous outlaw was expected to survive his latest
encounter:

"Curly Bill" not Dead.

From a gentleman who arrived from Galeyville yesterday, we learn that Curly Bill is rapidly recovering from the effects of his wound. Curly's escape from death was a miraculous one, the ball passed between the thorax and jugular vein without touching either. When the doctor examined the wound, Bill asked him what his chances for life were. The doctor replied that the chances were about even. "Then," exclaimed Bill, "I'm going to get well, for whenever I get an even chance I always come out ahead." Curly says his fighting days are over and he intends to return to Texas to see his old mother as soon as he recovers. He got off a witticism at the expense of his shooter, Wallace. "Boys," said he, "let Wallace go up to Tombstone. They'll turn out to meet him with a brass band!" It is a fact that there isn't much love in Tombstone for Curly, and no doubt Wallace would receive a popular ovation for his service in giving Curly a dose of lead, and thus incapacitating him from mischief for some weeks to come.-Journal.

Following the shooting in Galeyville, Curly Bill received wide coverage in the territorial newspapers—much as he had after the shooting of Fred White during his preliminary hearing in Tucson and the "treeing" of Charleston and Contention in January 1881. Like many of its contemporaries, the *Arizona Daily Star*, on May 26, 1881, published a detailed account of the shooting of Curly Bill:

"CURLY BILL"

This Noted Desperado "Gets It in
the Neck" at Galeyville.

The notorious "Curly Bill," the man who murdered Marshal White at Tombstone last fall, and who had been concerned in several other desperate and lawless affrays in Southeastern Arizona, has at last been brought to grief, and there is likely to be a vacancy in the ranks of our border desperadoes. The affair occurred at Galeyville Thursday. A party of eight or nine cow-boys, "Curly Bill" and his partner Jim Wallace among the number, were in town enjoying themselves in their usual manner, when Deputy Sheriff Breakenridge, of Tombstone, who was at Galeyville on business, happened along.

Wallace made some insulting remark to the deputy, at the same time time flourishing his revolver in an aggressive manner. Breakenridge did not pay much attention to this "break" of Wallace, but quietly turned around and left the party. Shortly after this "Curly Bill," who, it would seem, had a friendly feeling for Breakenridge, insisted that Wallace should go and find him and apologize for the insult given. This Wallace was induced to do, and after finding Breakenridge he made the apology, and the latter accompanied him back to the saloon where the cow-boys were drinking. By this time, "Curly Bill," who had drank just enough to make him quarrelsome, was in one of his most dangerous moods, and evidently desirous of increasing his record as a man-killer. He commenced to abuse Wallace, who, by the way, has some pretensions himself as a desperado and "bad man" generally, and finally said, "You d—d Lincoln County s— of a b——. I'll kill you anyhow." Wallace immediately went outside the door of the saloon, "Curly Bill" following close behind him. Just as the latter stepped outside, Wallace, who had meanwhile drawn his revolver, fired, the ball penetrating the left side of "Curly Bill's" neck and passing through came out the right cheek, not breaking the jaw-bone. A scene of the wildest excitement ensued in the town. The other members of the cow-boy party surrounded Wallace and threats of lynching him were made by them. The law-abiding citizens were in doubt what course to pursue. They did not wish any more bloodshed, but were in favor of allowing the lawless element to "have it out" among themselves. But Deputy Sheriff Breakenridge decided to arrest Wallace, which he succeeded in doing without meeting any resistance. The prisoner was taken before Justice Ellenwood, and after examination into the facts of the shooting he was discharged.

The wounded and apparrently dying desperado was taken into an adjoining building, and a doctor summoned to dress his wounds. After examining the course of the bullet, the doctor pronounced the wound dangerous, but not necessarily fatal, the chances for and against recovery being about equal. Wallace and "Curly Bill" have been partners and fast friends for the past five or six months, and so far as is known, there was no cause for the quarrel, it being simply a drunken brawl. A great many people in southeastern Arizona will regret that the termination was not fatal to one or both of the participants. Although the wound is considered very dangerous, congratulations at being freed from this dangerous character are now rather premature, as men of his class usually have a wonderful tenacity of life.

Uncorroborated accounts surfaced years later about Wallace's shooting of Curly Bill at Galeyville and have become part of Tombstone folklore. James Hancock claimed that Curly Bill was so drunk that

Milt Hicks and some others had disarmed him and were trying to get him out of town when he was shot.[8] Robert Boller, another old-timer, claimed that he would bring food to Curly Bill at Galeyville while he was still injured and in bed.[9] Melvin Jones also asserted that he had seen the cowboy around this time:

> I saw one was Curley Bill and the other "Russian Bill" Tattenbaum . . . . Curly had a bad wound on his face, was looking for a quiet place to rest and get well. We asked no questions, but he explained it all by saying: "A damned fool over a Galeyville let a six-shooter go off and the bullet hit me in the face." Curley was thin, boney-faced, sick . . . . [F]our weeks later . . . I met Curley Bill Graham riding a good horse, leading another packed with bed and camp outfit, his face well and looking healthy. We had a long talk.
>
> "I'm leaving Arizona forever," he told me. "If I try to stay, all I can expect is trouble. This damn name of Curley Bill and the notoriety that came from the accidental killing of Marshal White in Tombstone will get me blamed for every crime committed in Arizona or New Mexico, if I stay. Wouldn't make any difference how far I was away from the crime at the time" [10]

Reports of Curly Bill leaving the territory after being shot by Wallace were a recurring theme. One newspaper even wrote: "Curly says his fighting days are over and he intends to return to Texas to see his old mother as soon as he recovers. Nonetheless, a newspaper report from the *Arizona Weekly Star,* dated June 23, 1881, suggests that the notorious cowboy stayed in Galeyville while recuperating from his wound at least to the end of June: "'Curly Bill' is likely to recover from the wounds he recently received. He is reported as being able to walk about the streets of Galeyville, and will soon be in condition to

John Ringo has been accused with Curly Bill of killing the Haslett brothers during June 1881. However, neither man appears to have been involved in the deaths. Courtesy Dave Johnson.

again make it interesting for outlying settlements." Only rumor and innuendo place the notorious cowboy in Arizona during the months of July and August 1881.

In July 1881, Thomas Harper, became the first man legally hanged in Pima County. He was convicted of killing John Talliday in Ramsey's Canyon in the Huachuca Mountians during September 1880. Harper managed to have his first conviction overturned. Unfortunately he was convicted again in a second trial. Harper reportedly walked up the scaffold with a cool and jaunty demeanor. "He made no confession, but left a letter to Curly Bill," advising him "to take warning from him and not be too handy with a pistol and 'to stand a heap from a man before you kill him.'"[11] The letter was addressed to "Wm. H. Brocius, care G. W. Turner, San Simon."[12] Harper's letter probably reached Curly Bill, if he was still in Arizona, despite the fact that Turner was killed near Fronteras, Mexico in May 1881. Still, Curly Bill was not apparently ready to heed Thomas Harper's advice.

Decades later, in *Wyatt Earp,Frontier Marshal* (1931), Stuart Lake wrote that John Ringo and Curly Bill had killed two brothers in New Mexico named Haslett.[13] In reality, the Hasletts were killed in late June 1881 by a group of men, probably led by Jim Crane, after the Hasletts had killed Harry Head and Bill Leonard in New Mexico.[14] John Ringo likely was out of the territory at the time and was known to be in Texas by May 2, returning to Arizona from Missouri during July 1881.[15] Curly Bill was still nursing the wound that he had received in Galeyville and probably was in no shape to participate in killing the Haslett brothers. Therefore, contrary to Lake's assertions, it is doubtful that either man was involved in the deaths of the Haslett brothers.

9

FRONTERAS MASSACRE

Shortly before Curly Bill was shot by Jim Wallace at Galeyville, the border problems between the cowboys in Arizona and Mexican citizens in Sonora had escalated greatly, with deadly results. On May 13, 1881, Curly's friend George Turner, Galeyville butcher Al McAllister, and two others were attacked and killed by Mexicans near Fronteras, Mexico, while on a trip to acquire cattle to fulfill a contract to furnish beef to the army at Fort Bowie.[1] The Mexican citizens, led by Jose Juan Vasquez, suspected that the Americans had stolen the cattle in Mexico and were attempting to drive them into Arizona. When the Americans were surrounded by the Mexicans and ordered to surrender, they responded to the surrender demand with gunfire. In response, the Mexicans "returned with such deadly effect that three of the party fell dead, the other lived long enough to kill Vasquez," according to one witness.[2]

The Fronteras killings started rumors in Arizona that friends of McAllister might retaliate against the town of Fronteras. "Forty or fifty Cow-boys of bad character are ready for action between Los Animas and Galeyville," one army report declared in early June 1881.[3] Mexican federal troops prepared to repel the attack at the border. Newspapers in Arizona added to the tension along the border by publishing rumors that seventy cowboys were preparing to raid Mexico to avenge the death of the four cowboys who had been killed.[4] Additionally, rumors of unconfirmed cowboy attacks on Mexico began to surface even though the United States Army reported no evidence of raiding parties moving either to or from Mexico.[5]

Although Americans probably did threaten to retaliate against Fronteras for the killing of Curly Bill's friend George Turner and his party, the marauding cowboys never attacked the Sonoran town. Curly Bill was still recovering from his gunshot wound and reportedly was "able to walk about the streets of Galeyville;"[6] however, raiding Fronteras likely was not the foremost thing on his mind.

The following month, another gun battle erupted over cattle ownership between cowboys and Mexican citizens. The *Tombstone Nugget*, on August 3, 1881, reported that a party of Mexicans had raided into the United States, but before they could return to Mexico with the livestock, a party of ranchers intercepted them:

Cattle Thieves Routed

From Bob Clark, who recently returned from New Mexico, the NUGGET learns that about the 26th of last month, a party of Mexicans from Sonora made a raid into the Animas and adjoining valleys, and rounding up several hundred animals, started with them through the Guadalupe Pass [in New Mexico near the point where New Mexico, Arizona, and Sonora converge] for Mexico. The Mexicans numbered about thirty all told. The cattlemen organized about twenty in number, and pursuing the marauders, overtook them on the plains near the Pass. A running fight ensued, which resulted in the flight of the Mexicans, and the recovery of the cattle.

An old-timer later claimed that cowboys had raided Sonora to steal livestock and that the Mexicans were only trying to recapture the stolen herd. Fearing that they were outnumbered, the Mexicans were forced to abandon the herd and returned to Mexico empty-handed.[7] Some old-timers claimed that Curly Bill was involved in the ensuing gun battle with the Mexicans and that several Mexicans supposedly were killed.[8] Contemporary reports, however, failed to identify the men involved or whether anyone was killed in the fight.

A few days later, on July 27, 1881, another Mexican party was making its way north, heading for Arizona. The members of the party were travelling as a large pack train that intended to buy goods in Arizona and then take them back to Mexico to sell for a big profit. Unexpectedly, the Mexican pack train was ambushed. The *Epitaph* published the following account of the incident on August 5, 1881:

> An Interrupted Breakfast
>
> Report comes to us of a fresh outrage perpetrated by the cow-boys in Sonora. Early last Monday morning a party of sixteen Mexicans from the interior of Sonora on their way to this Territory to purchase goods and carrying $4000.00 for that purpose, stopped in a curve in the road at Las Animas, near Fronteras, to prepare their frugal breakfast. While busily engaged preparing their tortillas they were saluted with music of twenty rifles fired by cow-boys who lay in ambush awaiting them. The Mexicans took this as an invitation to leave and did not stand on the order of their going but left all their mules and pack saddles in which they carried their money for the purchase of goods. When they stopped running they were at Fronteras and their party was four short. The missing men are supposed to have been killed. The citizens of Babispe and troops are after the cow-boys and are disposed to take summary vengeance if they overtake them.

Curly Bill, although not implicated at the time, is commonly included among the men who participated in the ambush, which is popularly referred to as the Skeleton Canyon Massacre by many writers, even though the attack occurred a short distance from the Mexican town of Fronteras and fifty miles from Skeleton Canyon.[9] The Mexican government filed official protests with the Governor of Arizona, but little action was forthcoming. Meanwhile, the border raids continued to be reported in the newspapers. "The Arizona cowboys continue to have a high time on the Mexican border. They are represented to be in possession of large bands of cattle and horses, ready for the Texas market," the *San Francisco Evening Bulletin* commented.[10] In mid-August 1881, more border problems erupted, and four Americans, including Newman H. Clanton, the father of Phin, Ike, and Billy Clanton, were killed. Along with the elder Clanton, Dick Gray, Charles Snow, William Lang, and the wanted outlaw Jim Crane were killed.[11] The men were ambushed near the town of Gillespie, New Mexico, in the Guadalupe Canyon area. A Mexican party estimated to consist of twenty to thirty men, had ambushed the cowboys in the early morning hours while they were still asleep.

The survivors of the massacre and the relatives of the victims were in full agreement about one fact—the shooters were Mexican soldiers. Even Mexican sources alluded to the possibility that Mexican soldiers had committed the atrocity. The *Sacramento Daily Record-Union*, based on the remarks of General Adolfo Dominquez, spokesman for General Otero, commander of the Mexican troops on the Sonoran frontier, wrote, "It is not improbable that the killing in Guadalupe Canyon might have been done by Mexican regulars under Captain Carrillo, as they were headed in that direction. Carrillo has about fifty men in his company."[12] More talk of a large gang of cowboys massing in Arizona to seek vengeance for the killings again began to be heard. However, the rumors of a raiding party were quickly quashed. "The wild rumor of the vast crowd of determined men going out to avenge the dead men is all bosh. There were eleven men in the party and the object of their trip was to bury the dead," reported the *Arizona Weekly Citizen.*[13]

With the press declaring that the cowboy depredations along the border were at an all time high, the Governor began slowly to respond with inquiries about the situation in southeastern Arizona. In response, Joseph Bowyer, the manager of the Texas Consolidated Mining Company in Galeyville, sent a letter to the Governor of Arizona on September 17, 1881. It was later published by the *Tombstone Epitaph* on December 9, 1881:

Dear Sir: In reply to your inquiry concerning the Cowboys who are reported to have been and still are raiding the line of Sonora and Arizona, I will say: The gang who are known as cowboys are engaged in stock raising in the valley of San Simon and Cloverdale in the southeastern portion of Arizona, and from good authority I learn that the cattle, horses and sheep now controlled by said cowboys have been stolen from the citizens of Sonora and Arizona and New Mexico; they are reported to have about 300 head of cattle at or near Granite Gap in New Mexico and close to the line in Arizona. It is a well known fact that they are in the habit of making raids along the border. Until recently it has been custom to steal cattle and horses in Arizona and drive them into Sonora and New Mexico for sale; Consequently quite a traffic was keep up. . . . About a month ago the cowboys went across the border into Sonora, and seeing a good-sized pack train in charge of mexicans, laid ambush and at word of command, made a dash and succeeded in capturing the whole outfit, consisting of about $4000.00 in Mexican silver bullion, mescal, horses and cattle. One of the cowboys in relating to me the circumstances said it was the d--st lot of truck he ever saw. . . . There was three Mexicans killed in the affray. A notorious cowboy known as John R - offers to sell all the mutton the town can consume at $1 per head. No secrecy is observed in this kind of transaction. . . .

With news reports claiming that the San Simon cowboys had ambushed the Mexican party near Fronteras, the people of the territory now assumed that Curly Bill and other cowboys like John Ringo had been involved. The Governor relayed the information he received from Bowyer to the Secretary of State of the United States:

At Galeyville, San Simon and other points isolated from large places the cow-boy element at times very fully predominates, and the officers of the law at times are either unable or unwilling to control this class of outlaws, sometimes being governed by fear, at other times by hope of reward. At Tombstone, the County seat of Cochise County, I conferred with the sheriff of said county upon the subject of breaking up three bands of outlaws, and I am sorry to say he gave me little hope of being able in his department to cope with the power of the cow-boys. He represented to me that the deputy United States Marshal, resident of Tombstone, and city Marshal of same, and those who aid him (the deputy marshal) seemed unwilling to heartily cooperate with him (the sheriff) in capturing and bringing to justice these outlaws. In conversing with the deputy United States Marshal, Mr. Earp, I find precisely the same spirit of complaint existing against Mr. Behan (the sheriff) and his deputies. And back of this unfortunate fact, rivalry between the civil authorities, or unwillingness to work together in full accord in keeping the peace, I find two daily newspapers published in the city taking sides with the deputy marshal and the sheriff, respectively, each paper backing its civil clique and berating the other; and . . . peace loving citizens have no confidence in the willingness of the civil officers to pursue and bring to justice that element of outlawry so largely disturbing the sense of security, and so often committing highway robbery and smaller thefts. . . .[14]

Eventually, the reports made their way to the White House. In May 1882, Chester Arthur, the President of the United States, threatened to declare the Arizona Territory to be under martial law if the cowboys committing depredations did not disperse.[15]

Nothing but rumor and innuendo implicate Curly Bill in the border fights of July and August 1881. In fact, it is difficult to document his presence in the Arizona Territory during the period. Nonetheless, sometime in September 1881, Deputy Sheriff Breakenridge claimed that he encountered Curly Bill twice while in the countryside looking for stolen horses. On the first ocassion, Breakenridge met Curly Bill in the San Simon Valley on his way to Joe Hill's ranch.[16] Earlier in the day, the deputy had found two stolen horses in the valley. According to the deputy, he told Curly Bill that he had found two lost horses from the Chiricahua Cattle Company and that they had evidently strayed in there. Curly Bill helped round up the horses, but Breakenridge thought the notorious cowboy probably had stolen them. Another time, the deputy met Brocius at the McLaury ranch while looking for E. B. Gage's horse, which was believed to have been stolen by Sherman McMasters earlier in the month.[17] Breakenridge claimed that Ike Clanton had told him that the horse was at the McLaury ranch, and so Breakenridge went to the ranch and talked to Frank McLaury. "When I told him who I was, he asked me in, and on entering I found Curly Bill and some ten or twelve rustlers there with him," recalled Breakenridge.[18] Frank told Breakenridge that the horse was not there at the time but he would find the man that had it. Breakenridge stayed the night at the ranch, along with Curly Bill and several other cowboys. The next morning the horse was at the ranch and Breakenridge returned it to Contention City.

The following month, in early October 1881, the Indians in the area were making life in the outer regions of the county very dangerous. On Tuesday, October 4, 1881, rumors of a battle between the army and Indians at Dragoon Pass reached Tombstone, causing much excitement in the boom town. The following day, around noon, a large group of men from Tombstone that included Sheriff John Behan, Virgil Earp, Wyatt Earp, Morgan Earp, John Clum, George Parsons, and others, went out to aid the army in securing the county.[19] The next day the party crossed the Sulphur Springs Valley to the McLaury ranch. Parsons noted in his diary that at the ranch the men encountered the notorious Curly Bill:

Thursday October 6/81

. . . . At Mc L's was Arizona's most famous outlaw
@ the present time "Curly Bill" with two followers.
He killed one of our former Marshalls & to show
how we do things in Arizona I will say that our present
Marshall & said "C Bill" shook each other warmly by
the hand & hobnobbed together some time, when
said "C B" mounted his horse & with his two satellites
rode off—first though stealing a pair of spurs belonging
to one of our party as they couldn't be found after
their departure. "C B" was polite & considerate
enough though to sharply wheel his horse to one side
of my bridle which I had accidentally dropped. He's
not a bad looking man but looks very determined &
is not fully recovered from his Galeyville wound. It
was amusing to me to see with what marked deference
his two young followers acted towards their chief &
how they regarded us, affecting a devil-may-care,
braggadocio sort of manner.[20]

Parsons was somewhat shocked at how warmly Marshal Virgil
Earp treated Curly Bill, whom Parsons considered Arizona's most
famous outlaw. However, Curly Bill's reputation was based largely
on the killing of Fred White, a declared accident, and his "treeing" of
Charleston and Contention City in January 1881. Although Parsons
probably believed Curly Bill was involved in the border fights of 1881,
none of the men involved were ever publicly identified. More
importantly, none of the group of officers at the McLaury ranch, which
included federal, county, and local officers, arrested Curly Bill.
Consequently, it is clear that the notorious cowboy was not wanted
for the Bisbee robbery, as asserted by Lake in *Wyatt Earp, Frontier
Marshal,* or any other offense.[21] Yet, there is no doubt that Curly Bill
was publicly considered at this time, at least by some people, to be a
notorious rustler and desperado. A song written by Tombstone resident

George Parsons encountered Curly Bill at the McLaury Ranch and was somewhat shocked at the warm treatment the cowboy received from Tombstone Town Marshal Virgil Earp.

George Atwood and published by the *Tombstone Epitaph* on October 14, 1881, illustrates this point:

PROSPECTOR'S LAMENT
Tune- "Hat My Father Wore."
Composed and sung by Gordon Atwood

. . . Once I owned a bronco, and I bought
him for a song,
He wasn't very handsome,
but he carried me along;
But now I punch my burro all up and down the
hill,
For my bronco's gone to San Simon, to carry
Curly Bill . . . .

About a week later, nineteen cattle "went missing" in the Huachuca Moutains in Arizona, and rancher Eugene Edmonds filed a complaint for grand larceny against Curly Bill and a few others, who he suspected had stolen the cattle.[22] It's likely that the notorious cowboy had already started to ride to New Mexico before officers in Arizona could act. However, Curly's efforts to avoid being arrested were somewhat thwarted, at least temporarily, when he was arrested in New Mexico. It did not take long for news of the Brocius' arrest to make its way to Tombstone. "'Curly Bill,' who shot and killed City Marshal White about a year ago, is in jail in Lordsburg, New Mexico," the *Tombstone Nugget* reported on November 4, 1881. No details about the incident were provided; however, the *Silver City Enterprise*, on September 5, 1884, briefly referred to one occasion when Curly Bill was arrested in Lordsburg:

It was armed with one of them [a short-barrel shotgun], that Hora, deputy sheriff at Lordsburg, took in Curly Bill. Bill was riding out of a corral, and Hora stationed himself at a gate post. As Bill rode out, he covered him and told him to hold up his hands. Bill only glanced at the weapon and up went his hands.

Why the infamous cowboy was arrested is not known. It could not have been too serious, however, because as he was apparently released from the jail after a short time, possibly after only paying a fine. During this time the atmosphere in the smaller communities of both Arizona and New Mexico was changing, with deadly results for a few renegade cowboys. Within a week of Curly Bill's arrest in Lordsburg, a mob raided the jail at Shakespeare, lynching Sandy King and Russian Bill Tetenbuam, who were wanted for horse theft. On November 10, 1881, the *Arizona Weekly Star* reported the lynching of the two cowboys:

LYNCH LAW
For some weeks Shakespeare, N.M., and vicinity has been harassed by a number of horse thieves, who have been known as cowboys. The vigilant Tucker, better known as little Tuck, has been close on their trail. Sandy King was arrested some days ago and lodged in jail awaiting trial. Two days ago Russian Bill, who had stolen two horses, and had been traced to Sepa [Separ] Station, and, although he made his boasts that the man did not live who could take him in; yet, when he heard that Tuck was at the station he took refuge in the engine room of the water tank, and found no difficulty whatever in throwing up his hands when the word was given by Tuck. He was taken to Shakespeare, and yesterday morning, about 2 o'clock, a number of masked men took in the jail, and in a few minutes Russian Bill and Sandy King were no more. It is said Curly Bill had been arrested with Sandy King, but was lct out on paying a fine. 'Tis a pity he had not been held so that he could have accompanied his friends.

The small mining town of Shakespeare was only a few miles from Lordsburg. Therefore, despite Curly Bill's reported arrest in Lordsburg, it's also possible that the cowboy could have been taken to Shakespeare if the crime for which he was arrested had occurred at that town. The following month, on December 2, 1881, the Cochise County grand jury indicted Curly Bill for grand larceny.[23] The case was quickly entered on the District Court's docket on December 8, and a warrant was issued for his arrest on December 10.[24] The indictment was based on the complaint filed by Eugene Edmonds against Brocius and a few others:

> . . . William Broscius is accused by the Grand Jury of the County of Cochise, Territory of Arizona, by this Indictment found on the second day of December, A. D. 1881, of the crime of Grand Larceny committed as follows, to wit: the said William Broscius on or about the 22nd day of October A. D. 1881, and before the finding of this indictment, at the County of Cochise, Territory of Arizona, did unlawfully and feloniously steal[,] take and drive away certain meat cattle to wit, nineteen head of meat cattle—of the value of two hundred and eighty five ($285.00) dollars: Said meat cattle being then and there not the property of said William Broscius—but the personal property of one Eugene Edmonds.[25]

William Grounds, Zwing Hunt, and Led Moore were also indicted for this crime on December 2, 1881.[26] Likely unaware of the grand jury indictment, Curly Bill returned to Arizona and proceeded to make Charleston a lively place. "Curly Bill and three of his gang made things lively in Charleston Tuesday night [December 6, 1881]. They were visiting friends on the Bar bacomari and San Pedro, and ran into Charleston for a little pleasure," noted the *Tombstone Epitaph*.[27] Eight days later the *Tombstone Nugget* reported that Curly Bill was planning to leave the territory:

It is rumored, but lacks confirmation, that Curly Bill's crowd, consisting of Lit Moore, Zwing Hunt, Billy Grounds, alias the "kid," Jimmy Hughes, and Curly himself, have gathered together under the leafy boughs of the shady oak for the last time, in the vicinity of Shakespeare, N.M. We are inclined to doubt this report, from the fact that this gang were seen on the head of the Babacomari less than a week ago. Travel is increasing, and every man on the road is fixed for the bold, bad, rustler.[28]

The *Tombstone Nugget* doubted that the story of Curly's departure was true; however, the cowboy seemingly vanished from Arizona at this time. For the next two and a half months, no further sightings of Curly Bill were reported by the local newspapers. Only rumor and innuendo implicate the cowboy in crimes committed during this period.

In the District Court of the First Judicial District

OF THE

Territory of Arizona, in and for the County of Cochise.

TERRITORY OF ARIZONA
against

William Broscius
Defendant.

November Term,

*A. D. 188_1_.

William Broscius is

accused by the Grand Jury of the County of Cochise, Territory of Arizona, by this Indictment found on the Second *day of* December, *A. D. 188_1_,*
of the crime of —— Grand Larceny ——
committed as follows, to wit: The said William Broscius

on on or about the 22nd *day of* October *A. D. 188_1_, and before*
the finding of this Indictment, at the County of Cochise, Territory of Arizona,

did unlawfully and feloniously steal take and drive away certain neat cattle, to wit: Nineteen head of neat cattle of the value of Two hundred and eighty-five ($285.00) dollars: said neat cattle being then and there not the property of said William Broscius, but the personal property of one Eugene Edmunds.

The Cochise County grand jury indicted Curly Bill for grand larceny on December 2, 1881. Arizona Historical Society, George Chambers collection.

10

EARP BOYS VS. COWBOYS

On October 26, 1881, the most famous gunfight in the annals of the West took place. On one side were Chief of Police Virgil Earp, Wyatt and Morgan Earp, and Doc Holliday. On the other side were Ike and Billy Clanton and Tom and Frank McLaury, ranchers from out of town.[1] It was not a planned confrontation—it erupted spontaneously, the culmination of personal disputes that happened the night before.[2] When the smoke cleared, Frank McLaury was dead, and Tom McLaury and Billy Clanton lay on the ground mortally wounded. Also wounded in the affray were Morgan Earp, with a serious but not fatal shoulder wound, and Virgil Earp, who was hit in the calf of his right leg.

Despite the deadly result of the shootout, many people believed the Earp party's actions were justified because Virgil Earp was the town marshal. Thus, he had the duty and authority to disarm men carrying firearms in the town. However, once the local newspaper published testimony from the Coroner's Jury in the local newspaper, an equally large number of people began to consider the shooting to have been closer to cold-blooded murder. Newspaper correspondent Clara Brown wrote: "Opinion is pretty fairly divided as to the justification of the killing. You may meet one man who will support the Earps, and declare that no other course was possible to save their own lives, and the next man is just as likely to assert that there is no occasion whatever for bloodshed, and that this will be a 'warm place' for the Earps hereafter. At the inquest yesterday, the damaging fact was ascertained that only two of the cowboys were armed, it thus being a most unequal fight."[3] Following the proceedings of the Coroner's Jury, on October

Intersection of Fifth Street and Allen Street in Tombstone.

29, 1881, Wyatt Earp and Doc Holliday were arrested and placed in jail. Virgil and Morgan Earp were confined to their beds because they were injured.[4] Two days later, on October 31, 1881, a month-long hearing before Justice Wells Spicer began. The prosecution put on its case for nearly two weeks. Wyatt Earp took the stand as the first witness for the defense on November 16, 1881. Rather than present evidence by answering questions posed by his counsel and being cross-examined by the prosecutor, Wyatt chose to read a prepared statement into the court record. In his statement, Earp alleged that the Clanton party was part of the cowboy element that was causing cowboy depredations in the territory.[5] Wyatt further claimed that he had heard from others that several of the "cowboys" had threatened the lives of the Earps. "Old Man Winter, Charley Smith and three or four others had told us at different times of the threats to kill us made by Ike Clanton, Frank McLaury, Tom McLaury, Joe Hill and John Ringgold [Ringo]," Earp stated.[6] Interestingly, not one of the men whom Wyatt identified as having told the Earps of the prior threats testified at the hearing to corroborate Earp's allegations. Wyatt's prepared statement nevertheless succeeded in painting a dark picture of the Clantons and McLaurys as "desperate and dangerous men," who were "connected with outlaws, cattle thieves, robbers and murderers."[7] On November 30, 1881, Justice Wells Spicer, in a controversial ruling, rendered his decision: "The evidence taken before me in this case would not, in my judgment, warrant a conviction of the defendants by a trial jury of any offense whatever."[8] The charges against the Earps and Doc Holliday were dismissed.

The gunfight at the OK Corral and the subsequent release of the Earps and Doc Holliday began the Earp-Clanton feud. This conflict is sometimes referred to as the "Cowboy War," due largely to Wyatt's accusations that the Clantons and McLaurys were involved in the cowboy depredations occurring in the territory.[9] Ironically, Curly Bill, the man Parsons considered to be "Arizona's most famous outlaw," and who was suspected by many to be a leader of a gang of cowboys, was never mentioned by Earp as one of the men making threats against the Earp's lives.[10] Nevertheless, modern writers have had no problem placing Curly Bill in the center of the feud, even though there is little, if any, evidence of his involvement.

Rumors began to spread through Tombstone that friends of the Clantons and McLaurys had prepared a hit list that included the Earps, Doc Holliday, Tom Fitch, Wells Fargo agent Marshall Williams, Judge Spicer, and Mayor John Clum.[11] While some threats had been made to Judge Wells Spicer in a letter that was signed "A Miner," there was no indication that the cowboys had made out a death list that included those individuals [the Earps, Doc Holliday, Tom Fitch, Wells Fargo agent Marshall Williams, Judge Spicer, and John Clum].[12] Spicer felt the threats were coming from a rabble within the city, and not the cowboys.[13] About the rumored death threats, Tom Fitch commented that he had "never received a warning or menace from 'cow-boys' or anybody else" and felt perfectly safe.[14]

Two weeks after the charges against the Earps and Holliday were dismissed, on December 14, 1881, John Clum boarded a stage to Benson, the first leg of a trip to Washington, D.C., to visit his parents and son. After traveling about four miles, the stage was ordered to "halt," and several shots rang out.[15] The six horses pulling the stage were frightened by the shooting, and they burst into a gallop. About half a mile later, the driver gained control over the stage. Clum feared that the holdup was simply a sham and that its real purpose was to assassinate him. He quietly jumped from the coach and ran into the desert. Taking no chances, Clum hiked alone through the desert to the Grand Central Mill, near Contention City. Meanwhile, back in Tombstone it was feared that Clum may have been killed, but the mill superintendent contacted Tombstone by telephone to advise people there that the mayor was safe. Nevertheless, the *Epitaph* claimed "the affair of Wednesday night was intended for the murder of John P. Clum, we are fully satisfied."[16] The *Nugget*, on the other hand, thought that it was more likely that Clum overreacted to a botched stage robbery.[17]

Whether the attackers wanted to assassinate Clum or were robbers who intended to take the cashbox is not known—the perpetrators were never identified. Nevertheless, Curly Bill is

John Clum and his first wife, Mary. Clum was the founder of the *Tombstone Epitaph* newspaper and mayor of Tombstone during the turbulent year of 1881. He was a staunch supporter of the Earp brothers.

occasionally named as one of the assailants who attacked the stage carrying Clum. Stuart Lake, Wyatt's biographer, later claimed that "Ike Clanton, Frank Stilwell, Curly Bill, John Ringo, Billy Claiborne, Hank Swilling, and Phin Clanton had led the attack to assasinate Mayor Clum." [18] No evidence has ever been found or presented that links Curly Bill to the incident or identifies the actual the men that attacked the stage that night, however.

Two weeks later, on the night of December 28, 1881, Deputy U. S. Marshal Virgil Earp was shot twice in an ambush while walking along a Tombstone street. [19] It was thought at first that he might die from his injuries. He survived, but, with a large section of bone removed from his arm, he would be crippled for life. George Parsons, a friend of Mayor John Clum and an Earp supporter, was in town at the time Virgil was shot. "It is surmised that Ike Clanton, Curly Bill, and [Will] McLaury did the shooting," wrote George Parsons in his diary. [20] Parsons' comments, however, were based on nothing more than unsubstantiated rumors. Nothing had been heard of Curly Bill since the *Nugget* had reported that he was leaving the territory three weeks before. Morevoer, the cowboy was not implicated in Virgil Earp's shooting at the time. [21]

Two days following the attempt on Virgil Earp's life, the *Epitaph*, on December 30, 1881, published a lengthy article with information attributed to Mrs. J. C. Colyer, who had recently been in Arizona. Mrs. Colyer declared that Ringo and Clanton were the "Chiefs of the Cow-boy's gang," and that Ringo and Clanton had planned the raids that other cowboys carried out. [22] Like Wyatt's prepared statement read to Spicer's court in November 1881, Mrs. Colyer's comments made no reference whatsoever to Curly Bill being a leader of the cowboys. Although Curly Bill was still considered a notorious cowboy by many in Tombstone, the public now perceived John Ringo and Ike Clanton to be the leaders of the cowboys following the gunfight near the OK Corral. Both men were considered key antagonists of the Earps.

On January 6, three bandits robbed the Sandy Bob stage between Hereford and Bisbee. [23] Before riding off with "$6,500 in

Ike Clanton was not armed during the Gunfight near the OK Corral and was the only surviver of the Clanton-McLaury group.

specie [coin] and currency, being sent over to pay the Copper Queen miners and workmen" in Bisbee, an unmasked outlaw, who throughout the robbery did all the talking, threatened to kill the driver of the stagecoach if he did anything to identify any of them.[24] At the time, the robbers were not identified, though unsupported rumors implicated Ringo in the robbery.[25] Warrants were nevertheless later issued for the true suspects—Pony Deal, Al Tiebot, and Charles Haws.[26] Wells, Fargo & Co. employee Charles Bartholomew had named the three as being the highwaymen who stole the $6,500 from the stagecoach.

Despite not being identified as one of the holdup men at the time or being charged with the crime, in *Wyatt Earp, Frontier Marshal,* Stuart Lake alleged that Curly Bill was involved in the holdup.[27] According to Lake, before Curly Bill left the scene, he took Bartholomew's Wells, Fargo shotgun. Lake's story, which orginated with Wyatt Earp, was entertaining to modern readers, but Curly Bill most likely did not take part in the robbery.[28] The cowboy, without a doubt, did not take Bartholomew's shotgun, which was thought to have been taken by the robbers. A Mexican later discovered the weapon out in the desert near the road where the robbery took place.[29]

The day after the Sandy Bob stage was robbed, two masked men held up a second stage as it traveled between Contention City and Tombstone. This time, the desperadoes rode off with $1500 and a fancy pair of pistols owned by James Hume, the Wells, Fargo chief detective. Once again, there was little evidence identifying the suspected outlaws, and Curly Bill was not implicated at the time. Still, Lake claimed that "Pony Deal and Curly Bill had pulled off this second robbery."[30] According to Lake, "Curly Bill took from Jim Hume a pair of ivory-handled, gold mounted six-guns, and joked about his growing collection of Wells-Fargo weapons."[31] In actuality, Alex Arnold, who was purported to be the new owner of Jim Hume's fancy pistols, and Pink Truly were later suspected of committing the crime.[32]

On January 24, 1882, Wyatt and a posse rode out of Tombstone toward Charleston with federal warrants issued by Judge Stilwell vaguely described as for "divers persons."[33] Lake later claimed, without substantiation, that Earp had gone to Charleston to arrest Pony Deal and Curly Bill.[34] However, Wyatt's underlying purpose was to find Ike and Phin Clanton, whom he suspected of ambushing his brother Virgil. Earp's mission was largely thwarted by John Ringo, who had learned of the lawman's intention and rode to Charleston to warn the Clantons of Earp's plan.[35]

After receiving assurances that no Earps would be involved, on January 30, 1882, Isaac and Phineas Clanton surrendered to a "neutral" posse led by Charles Bartholomew, a Wells, Fargo shotgun guard. At Tombstone, the brothers learned, to their surprise, that they were not being accused of stage robbery or cattle rustling, as they had been led to believe, but were being charged with assault to commit murder on Virgil Earp.[36] A preliminary hearing was promptly convened and Ike and Phin were released on bail.[37] The charges against the men were later dismissed after a trial.[38]

On March 18, 1882, Wyatt and Morgan were at "Campbell & Hatch's billiard parlor, on Allen street between Fourth and Fifth," when a shot blasted through the window pane of the back door, hitting Morgan.[39] "The bullet entered the right side of the abdomen, passing through the spinal column, completely shattering it, emerging on the left side, passing the length of the room and lodging in the thigh of Geo. A. B. Berry, who was standing by the stove, inflicting a painful flesh wound," the *Epitaph* later reported.[40] A second shot hit the wall above Wyatt Earp's head.[41] Morgan fell instantly and died within an hour.

The day after the shooting, Coroner H. M. Matthews empaneled a jury to investigate the circumstances of Morgan's death. After hearing testimony from several witnesses, the jurors determined that the killer was most likely one of a group of conspirators—Pete Spence, Frank Stilwell, "John Doe" Freeze or Freis (later identified as Frederick Bode), and two Indians or half-breeds, one named Charlie, the other unknown.[42] The juror's based their conclusion in large part on damning statements made by Marietta Spence, Pete Spence's wife, who obviously wanted to see her husband behind bars. The jury did not determine which of the conspirators actually pulled the trigger on the revolver from which the fatal bullet was fired, nor did they propose a motive for the attack. The Earps had been involved in the arrest of Spence and Stilwell for stage robbery the previous September, and this could have inspired the accused parties to assault the lawmen.[43] It is also reasonable that the same parties that killed Morgan were responsible for shooting Virgil in late December 1881.

Curly Bill is often accused of participating in Morgan Earp's killing even though there is no evidence linking him to the murder. Lake later claimed that Curly Bill had fired a round at Wyatt, but the shot deflected when it hit the glass.[44] Over forty years later, Wyatt Earp identified the men that he believed had murdered his brother:

> The men who murdered my brother were Curly Bill, Ringo, Stillwell, Hank Swelling, and the Mexican Florentine. I was told by their lawyer that I must be careful that they were going to assassinate us all. I don't care to tell who the lawyer was who told me as he was a good friend of mine. And at the same time was handling the other side.[45]

Wyatt's claim is questionable considering the testimony of Briggs Goodrich, who testified before a coroner's jury about the conversation that he had with Earp. The *Tombstone Epitaph* reported Goodrich's testimony on March 23, 1882:

> By the way, (Goodrich speaking to Earp) John Ringo wanted me to say to you, that if any fighting came up between you all, he wanted you to understand that he would have nothing to do with it; that he was going to look after himself, and anybody else could do the same. I think that from what Frank Stilwell said, that there would be trouble. He said there was some boys in town who would toe the mark, and the worst of it was the Earps would think he was in it, as they do not like him. I told him I would tell them the same for for

him as I had for John Ringo, and he said, no, that he would rather die than let them know he cared a damn what they thought. I advised him to keep off the streets at night, and then he would be able to prove an alibi.

In contrast to Wyatt's claim, Goodrich's sworn testimony indicates that he did not tell Earp the names of anyone he suspected might attempt to kill the Earps. Thus, it is unlikely that Briggs Goodrich told Wyatt Earp that Curly Bill was involved in the murder of Morgan Earp.

Virgil Earp and his wife Allie boarded a train at Contention City, with Colton, California, as their ultimate destination. They were escorted as far as Tucson by Wyatt Earp, Warren Earp, Doc Holliday, Sherman McMasters, and "Turkey Creek" Jack Johnson, all heavily armed. When their train reached Tucson on the evening of the 20th, the Earp party came upon Ike Clanton and Frank Stilwell at the station. Ike Clanton, who had been in Tucson for over two weeks, was expecting Milt McDowell of Charleston to arrive in town to testify as a witness in Jerry Barton's trial before the district court. Stilwell had been subpoenaed by the district court.[46] After seeing the Earp party, Clanton told Stilwell that the Earps were at the station and that he should make a run for it. Frank Stilwell could not evade the Earps, however, and his body was found the next day, shot several times.[47]

The Earp party quickly traveled back to Tombstone, where Wyatt Earp was informed that an arrest warrant from Tucson had been issued for him and the rest of his party. The men packed some things and prepared to leave the town. Sheriff Behan attempted to stop Wyatt Earp and his party. However, Earp refused to surrender, and Sheriff Behan was forced to back down.[48]

The Earp party rode out of Tombstone on March 21, 1882. Rather than galloping their horses for the safety of the border, Wyatt Earp and his men the next morning rode over to Pete Spence's wood camp looking for Spence and a man named Indian Charlie.[49] Wyatt Earp had personal wrongs to avenge, and he was intent on settling the score with the men who he believed killed his brother Morgan.

The Earp party reached Pete Spence's wood camp the next day before noon, and the first man they encountered was Theodore Judah, a hired hand at the wood camp. After talking to Judah, the party learned that Spence was probably in Tombstone, but a Mexican named Florentino Cruz was nearby. Judah watched as the Earp party rode toward Florentino's location. Moments later, Judah heard several gunshots echo in the distance. The next day, Cruz's lifeless body was found riddled by gunshots.[50]

Although modern writers occasionally implicate Curly Bill in the events that occurred during the Earp-Clanton feud from December 1881 to March 1882, there is little evidence that the notorious cowboy took part in any of the incidents. The cowboy was still wanted for grand larceny and Sheriff John Behan, during February 1882, sent a deputy to El Paso to search for Curly Bill in response to reports that he had been seen there.[51] The deputy came home without his man, but the sheriff wouldn't have sent him so far afield if there was good information floating around that Curly was still in Cochise County. With Curly Bill's whereabouts very much in doubt, in late February 1882, rumors spread to Tombstone that Curly Bill was dead. Nonetheless, the report of the desperado's passing provided neither any details of where he had supposedly died nor any details of how the cowboy met his demise. Consequently, few people, if any, in Tombstone considered the rumor to be trustworthy and it was quickly dismissed as a canard. "The reported death of 'Curly Bill' is, we are informed by reliable parties, without foundation," wrote the *Tombstone Nugget*.[52]

A month after Curly Bill's rumored death was dispelled, tension was running high in Arizona following the deaths of Morgan Earp, Frank Stilwell, and Florentino Cruz. The Earp party was on the run, with a sheriff's posse on their trial, when another claim was made that the notorious Curly Bill Brocius was killed. Unlike the earlier rumors of the cowboy's death, this claim was much harder for the public to dismiss—largely due to the fact that the *Tombstone Epitaph* firmly championed the claim. Still, other newspapers like the *Arizona Daily Star* and the *Tombstone Nugget* did not believe the rumor to be true.

Billy Clanton and Tom and Frank McLaury in their coffins after the
gunfight near the OK Corral.

Frank McLaury was armed during the gunfight and died defending himself.

Tom McLaury was not armed during the gunfight and was killed by a shotgun blast fired by Doc Holliday.

11

BATTLE AT BURLEIGH SPRINGS

On March 24, 1882, two days after Florentino Cruz was shot and killed, the Earp party rode to a spring in the Whetstone Mountains, about twenty miles from Tombstone. Wyatt reportedly had arranged a noon rendezvous at that location with Dan Tipton, a friend who was bringing badly needed funds to the wanted men. As the Earp party neared the spring, they were surprised to find men camping at the watering hole. When they were within thirty yards of the spring, gunfire erupted.[1] Wyatt Earp stood his ground and fired back at the opposing men while everyone else in the Earp party turned and fled at the sound of the first shots being fired. Finding himself fighting alone, Earp fired at his assailants, and he successfully retreated from the makeshift battlefield, joining his friends a short distance away.[2]

A few hours later, from their new vantage point, the Earp party observed two men approaching the spring. Although Wyatt believed that the new arrivals likely were sent to meet him, the Earp party was not in a position to warn the two messengers, "Dick Wright, better known in Tombstone as Whistling Dick, and Tony Kraker," of the cowboys' encampment.[3] As Wright and Kraker neared the spring, "they were suddenly confronted by four men with leveled guns pointed directly at them."[4] The cowboys, however, lowered their guns and invited the men to join them once the visitors told them that they were hunting for a mule that had strayed. Around the campfire that evening, the four men told Wright and Kraker about their skirmish with the Earp party earlier in the day. According to Wright and Kraker, "They said that not one of the Earp party charged but Wyatt, the balance all running away. Wyatt dismounted and fired his gun at them but without effect."[5] Later that evening, "the cowboys rode off," and Wright and Kraker "also departed in search of the Earp party."[6] After traveling a short distance, they found Wyatt Earp, who told them his version of the earlier battle and, more suprisingly, said that he had killed the notorious Curly Bill Brocius during the fight.[7]

Following the fight at the spring, information began slowly to trickle to nearby towns. In Contention City, only fourteen miles from the site of the shootout, Tucsonan George Hand the next morning heard rumors of the fight. On March 25, 1882, Hand recorded the hearsay information in his diary: "Report says four cowboys encamped at a spring met the Earp party and had a fight. Texas Charlie [Texas Jack Vermillion] had his horse killed and W. Earp was shot."[8] News also reached Tombstone by the morning of March 25, 1882. "Rumors of a battle and four of the Earp party killed received this a.m.," noted George Parsons in his diary.[9] Throughout the day, dispatches containing wild rumors and unsubstantiated statements were sent from Tombstone to Tucson and other Arizona cities. The *Tucson Citizen* published one such report on March 26, 1882:

> Tombstone. March 25. There is no further information of fight. The Earp party is supposed to be in the Whetstone Mountains closely followed by Behan and twelve deputies. Fin Clanton, Curly Bill, Ringold and fourteen other cowboys in pursuit of the Earp party. We are expecting news of a fight any hour.

Nothing was known of Curly Bill's whereabouts during the prior three months. No newspapers reported Curly Bill's presence in any town or place in Arizona, New Mexico, or anywhere else. In fact, a month earlier, in February 1882, Sheriff Behan, believing that the cowboy had left the territory, sent a deputy to serve an arrest warrant on Curly Bill in El Paso.[10] Although the deputy did not find the wanted desperado, Behan wouldn't have sent the deputy to El Paso unless he thought Brocius had left Arizona and was now in Texas.

Moreover, there is little, if any, evidence that the notorious cowboy was even involved in the Earp-Clanton feud. He was not accused of making threats against the Earps prior to the gunfight near the OK Corral, and only innuendo places him in Tombstone when Virgil and Morgan were shot. Why would a wanted man like Curly join the fray between the Earps and Clantons at this point? More importantly, the battle at the spring happened on March 24 and had already occurred when the dispatch alleging that Curly was riding with a cowboy posse originated in Tombstone the next day. In actuality, the reported sighting of Curly was only an unsupported rumor—one of many that spread throughout the territory that day.

Writers often have stated that there were two posses—one led by cowboys and the other led by Sheriff John Behan—chasing the Earp party at this time.[11] In reality, however, there was only one posse after the Earp party—Sheriff John Behan's posse consisting of over twenty men. Although Behan's posse did include John Ringo and Phin Clanton and also men from Tombstone, Curly Bill Brocius (who was still wanted for grand larceny) was not part of the group.[12] On March 24, Behan's posse left Contention City around the time the battle at the spring occurred, and it headed for Kinnear's ranch at the far end of the Whetstone Mountains. Rather than heading toward the spring in search of the Earp party, the posse had left Contention City in the opposite direction, away from the spring. The posse spent the night of March 24 at Kinnear's ranch before returning to Contention City the next evening.[13]

More dispatches based on rumor and speculation began to be received in Tucson on March 25, 1882. The *Arizona Daily Star* noted that "Under Sheriff Coleman received a dispatch to the effect that Wyatt Earp was mortally wounded and Texas Jack killed."[14] Later that day Ike Clanton received a telegram in Tucson from John Chenowith: "It is reported that four of the Earps are killed. Another report says one of the Earp party and Curly Bill are killed. There is nothing certain yet."[15] Although there were many stories of what was occurring, none was corroborated with supporting evidence. By the afternoon of March 25, a claim that Curly Bill was killed in the fight finally reached Tombstone. Wyatt Earp later claimed that he sent a letter to the *Tombstone Epitaph* detailing the fracas. At Tombstone, George Parsons added the following comments to his diary: "I got strictly private news though later that 'Curly Bill' has been killed at last by the Earp party, and none of the latter hurt."[16] Toward the afternoon and evening of March 25, a "reliable man just in from Burleigh Springs" told a *Tombstone Epitaph* reporter that Curly Bill had been killed.[17] A dispatch was sent to the *Arizona Daily Star*, which published the following account the next day:

> Reported Fight.
> [Special Dispatch to the Star.]
> Tombstone, March 25.- An Epitaph reporter interviewed a reliable man just in from Burleigh Springs, eight miles south of this city. He states that a desperate fight took place there last night between six men of the Earp party and nine cowboys, headed by the notorious Curly Bill, who killed Marshal White of Tombstone. The cowboys ambushed the Earps as they were approaching the spring and poured a deadly fire into them, wounding one man slightly and killing a horse. The Earps returned the fire and then charged upon the cowboys, who ingloriously ran, leaving Curly Bill dead upon the field.
> [This dispatch is mere rumor, and is not credited.-Ed. Star] [18]

Although the editor of the *Star* printed the reported fight, he noted that the story was only a rumor and not corroborated. The editor further commented, "The telegraphic dispatch from Tombstone, which we publish, lacks credibility. It is not believed that such a one-sided encounter has taken place; besides Curly Bill is known to be in another part of the country."[19] Clearly, based on the above statement, there was a general belief among the public at the time that Curly Bill had left Arizona prior to the shootout. On March 25, 1882, the

Tombstone Epitaph published a more detailed article, which alleged that a fight occurred at Burleigh Springs between the Earp party and nine fierce cowboys, led by the daring and notorious Curly Bill:

BATTLE OF BURLEIGH

The Earp Party Ambushed
by Curly Bill and Eight Cowboys.

A Hand to Hand Encounter
in Which Curly Bill Is Killed.

The town has been full of reports the last two or three days as to the whereabouts of the Earp party, and their probable movements. No sooner had one report got well under way than another was issued which contradicted it. There has been marching and countermarching by the sheriff and his posse until the community has become so used to the ring of spurs and clank of steel that comparatively little attention is paid to the appearance of large bodies of horsemen in the streets. Yesterday afternoon the sheriff with a large force started down the road toward Contention, possibly to follow up the report that the party had been seen in the Whetstone mountains, west of the San Pedro river, with their horses completely fagged out and the men badly demoralized. This, like so many other reports, was as baseless as the fabric of a dream.

The Battle of Burleigh Springs
Yesterday afternoon as the sun was descending low down the western horizon, had a person been traveling on the Crystal or Lewis Spring road towards the Burleigh Spring, as our informant was, he would have seen one of the most desperate fights between the six

men of the Earp party and nine fierce cowboys led by
the daring and notorious Curly Bill, that ever took
place between opposing forces on Arizona soil.
Burleigh Springs is about eight miles south of
Tombstone and some four miles east of Charleston,
near the mine of that name, and near the short road
from Tombstone and Hereford. As our informant,
who was traveling on horseback leisurely along toward
the Burleigh, came to a slight elevation in the road
about a half mile south thereof, he observed a party
of six men ride down to the spring from the east, where
they all dismounted. They had not much more than
got well upon their feet when there rose up at a short
distance away

Nine Armed Men

who took deadly aim and fired simultaneously at the
Earp party, for such the six men proved to be.
Horrified at the sight that like a lightning stroke flashed
upon his vision, he instinctively stopped and watched
for what was to follow. Not a man went down under
the murderous fire, but like a thunderbolt shot from
the hand of Jove the six desperate men charged upon
their assailants like the light brigade at Balaklava, and
when within easy reach returned the fire under which
one man went down never more to rise again. The
remaining eight fled to the brush and regained their
horses when they rode away towards Charleston as
if the King of Terrors was at their heels in hot pursuit.
The six men fired but one volley and from the close
range it is supposed that several of the ambushed
cowboys were seriously if not fatally wounded.

The Six Men

returned to their horses where one was found to be in
the agony of death, he having received one of the
leaden messengers intended for his rider. The party

remained at the spring for some time refreshing themselves and their animals when they departed going southerly as if they were making for Sonora.

The Dead Man Curly Bill

After the road was clear our informant rode on and came upon the dead man, who, from the description given, was none other than Curly Bill, the man who killed Marshal White in the streets of Tombstone, one year ago last September [October 1880]. Since the above information was obtained it has been learned that friends of Curly Bill went out with a wagon and took the body back to Charleston where the whole affair has been kept a profound secret, so far as the general public is concerned.

This overactive tale started a frenzy of news reports concerning the event. Some declared that Curly Bill was dead, others that Wyatt Earp was wounded. Nevertheless, the *Tombstone Nugget* strongly doubted that Curly Bill was killed by the Earp party. In an effort to get to the truth, the *Nugget* sent out reporters and, on March 26, 1882, published the following account based on an informant, likely Dick Wright or Tony Kraker, who claimed to have been told the account by Wyatt Earp:

THE TRUE BUSINESS

Conflicting Accounts of the Fight
in the Whetstones.
Wyatt Earp Believed to be
seriously Wounded.

The weak attempt of the Epitaph to gain a little temporary notoriety, by publishing an account of an imaginary fight between the Earps and the cowboys, did not meet with the hearty reception from the public which its projectors, no doubt, hoped for. The glaring improbability of the whole article was so patent to all, that the only effect produced was an expression of disgust at the puerile attempt to trifle with the feelings of an already excited and aroused community, and none were found so credulous as to place the slightest confidence in the truth and veracity of the silly canard.

The Nugget, knowing the movements of the Sheriff's posse in their attempt to effect the arrest of fugitives from justice is a question in which the entire communtiy feels a vital and absorbing interest, has spared neither trouble nor expense in its efforts to present its readers with the full and true account of the same.

From a party, whose name the Nugget is not at liberty to publish, the following version of the fight was obtained: Our informant had an appointment to meet the Earp party at a certain spring in the Whetstone Mountains, about fifteen miles distant from Contention at noon on Friday. He rode up to the spring, which is situated in a canyon, at the appointed time, and was confronted by three cowboys with drawn weapons, who ordered him to dismount, and demanded the cause of his presence there. He told them he was in search of a stray horse, and had come to the spring, thinking that a likely place to find the lost animal. The cowboys, evidently believing the story, abandoned

THEIR HOSTILE ATTITUDE

and invited the stranger to camp there and prepare his dinner, which invitation was accepted. While thus engaged, the cowboys rode off, and soon our informant also departed in search of the Earp party. He had proceeded but a short distance when he came upon Wyatt Earp. Wyatt informed him that some hour previous they (the Earp party) had come to the spring in pursuance of the appointment. They had approached within thirty yards, when they discovered four cowboys camped there. The latter recognized the intruders and firing from both parties began about the same time. One shot from the cowboys passed through the clothing of McMasters, just grazing his side; another killed Texas Jack's horse; a third knocked the pommel off Wyatt Earp's saddle; while another cut the straps of the field-glass carried by McMasters. The volley fired by the Earp party apparently did not take effect. The latter then started to retreat, Texas Jack jumping up behind one of the party. As they turned to run, one of the cowboys, whom Wyatt Earp believes to have been

THE NOTORIOUS CURLY BILL,

in a spirit of bravado, jumped out from behind a rock, when Wyatt turned in his saddle and fired, and the reckless cowboy fell to the ground. The Earp party retired behind an adjacent hill and halted. They were in a position commanding a view of the spring, and shortly after the fight saw a wagon come to the place, and as Wyatt believes, carry away the dead body of Curly Bill. They also saw the informant of the Nugget when he arrived at the spring, but were not in a position to warn him of the presence of the cowboys. Our informant was most positive and emphatic in the statement that neither Wyatt Earp, nor any one of the party, was wounded.

Desirous of presenting its readers with the latest and most authentic information in regard to the lamentable condition of affairs which now prevails, the Nugget last night dispatched couriers to Contention and Charleston, with instructions to ascertain, if possible, the authenticity of the foregoing statements:

THE ANNEXED TELEGRAMS,
it will be observed, in a measure corroborate what
has been related. The following was received from
Charleston at 8:40 p. m.

It is certain that the Earp party have had a
fight near the Whetstone Mountains. Wyatt stood
fire and was struck with a ball in the breast. The
balance ran. Texas Jack had a horse shot. Impossible
to ascertain anything in regard to Curly Bill.

The first dispatch from Contention was
received at 8: p. m., and is as follows:

Behan and posse just arrived. Four of the
posse were encountered by the Earps, yesterday,
while at dinner. Several shots were exchanged. The
Earps fled, except Wyatt, who dismounted and
emptied his shotgun. Texas Jack's horse was killed.
Wyatt is supposed to be wounded. The posse were
unhurt.

The latest from Contention was received at 1
a. m. this morning, and may be considered absolutely
reliable. It is as follows:

The Earps were withing thirty yards of the
camp when the fight commenced. The shooting
commenced in the Whetstones, twelved miles distant.
Wyatt, without a doubt, is wounded. Sheriff Behan is
still here. He states that four men engaged in the fight
had no connection with his posse. There is much
excitement here, but the report of the killing of Curly
Bill is not credited. The Earp party were seen from
the train, three miles below here, this afternoon.

From the story reproduced above, an amalgam of rumor and
anonymous tips, we can glean some probable facts: A skirmish between
the Earp party and some "cowboys" did take place, but in the foothills
of the Whetstone Mountains (probably at Mescal Spring), not at

Burleigh Springs on the east side of the San Pedro River.[20] The men who exchanged shots with the Earp party were not posse members. Moreover, the account of the killing of Curly Bill originated with Wyatt Earp. As is to be expected when the information is all secondhand or thirdhand, the story of the tussle at the spring, as described by the *Nugget*'s informant who claimed to have talked with Wyatt Earp, is questionable in several respects. Of concern is the assertion by Wyatt that Curly Bill left a secure position behind a boulder and presented himself to Earp's gun, almost like he committed suicide. Then, apparently within minutes, a wagon miraculously appeared to haul Curly away. In reality, it would have taken a fair amount of time for one of the "cowboys" to ride to a ranch or town, obtain a wagon and team, and bring the conveyance back to the remote fight scene. Also, each of the men at the spring presumably had a saddle horse. Why not tie Curly's body across his saddle and take him out of the mountains the easy way? Finally, the people at Charleston and Contention City had no knowledge, either firsthand or by rumor, that Curly Bill had been killed by the Earp party.[21] On March 27, 1882, the *Epitaph* printed yet another "Burleigh" gunfight article:

BATTLE OF BURLEIGH

Two Versions of the Fight.

You Pays Your Money and You
Takes Your Choice.

In the account of the Battle of Burleigh given in Saturday's EPITAPH, the facts were faithfully given to our reporter, and upon later inquiries being made it is asserted upon what is considered good authority that it was correct in all essential points other than the locality, which, it is stated, was purposely misrepresented. It has since been learned that in the fire of the cowboys that Wyatt Earp received seven shots through his clothes, but was not scratched by a bullet, and that one shot went through McMasters' clothes, just creasing his person, but doing no serious damage whatever. The horse of Texas Jack was shot dead and the pommel of one of the saddles was shot off, which completes the list of casualties to the Earp party, so far as can be learned. It is still asserted that

CURLY BILL WAS KILLED

upon the return fire of the new-comers at the spring. His death is stoutly denied by the cowboy party, however, who say that he is not in this part of the country, while the other side as positively assert its truth. It would seem that the Earp party, every man of whom knows Curly Bill as well as they would know their reflections in a glass, ought to know whether it was him or his double, if he has one.

THE COWBOY VERSION

On Friday last, Dick Wright, better known in Tombstone as "Whistling Dick," and Tony Kraker, were out on the mesa west of Drew's ranch, below Contention, in search of strayed mules, and just at evening they rode down to the spring when they were suddenly confronted by four men with leveled guns pointed directly at them. Tony sung out, "What are you doing there, you lop-eared Missourian?" This original salutation disarmed the cowboys, who lowered their guns and invited Tony and Dick to get down and make themselves at home, which they did. Sitting around the camp fire the four cowboys told them their version of the story, which was as follows: They said that they were camped at the spring, when they saw the Earp party ride down, and not knowing how they stood with them they thought that they would

GIVE THEM A SHOT

just for luck, so they blazed away and shot off the

pommel of Wyatt Earp's saddle and killed the horse that Texas Jack was riding. They said that not one of the Earp party charged upon them but Wyatt, the balance all rushing away. Wyatt dismounted and fired his gun at them but without effect. Texas Jack is said to have jumped up behind one of the other boys a la Mexicana, and off they went as rapidly as they could.

These are about as near the two sides of the fight as can be got at this time.

A LUDICROUS SCENE.

The other side, who claim to have killed Curly Bill and remained masters of the situation, say that after the battle was over and they had returned to their horses, and Texas Jack had found his beautiful pony dead, one that had carried him from Texas to Tombstone, and over many a weary and scorching plain in Texas, New Mexico and Arizona, [and Texas Jack] knelt down by the side of the faithful beast, unbared [uncovered] his angered brow, and there, upon his bended knees, took a deep and desperate oath to avenge the poor animal's death. This incident aptly illustrates the old saying that "It is but a step from the sublime to the ridiculous."

With the foregoing statements the reader will be able to draw some conclusion that may satisfy his or her mind about the late battle of so-called Burleigh.[22]

Did Wyatt have a reason to state that he killed Curly Bill if he did not do so? Yes—money. Rumors had circulated that prominent rancher Henry C. Hooker and the local cattleman's association placed an under-the-table $1,000 reward on Curly Bill's head. This reward report very likely was false (if it were true it would have been another good reason for Curly to leave the region); however, if Wyatt believed it, he could have cooked up the "I killed Curly Bill" scenario to obtain some cash—which he badly needed to finance his escape from Arizona. Whatever his motive, immediately after the Whetstone Mountain fracas, Wyatt and his companions headed toward Hooker's Sierra Bonita Ranch, located about sixty miles north of Tombstone. They arrived at the Sierra Bonita on March 27, where they were greeted warmly by its proprietor. The *Nugget,* on March 31, 1882, published a story describing the rumored payoff for Curly Bill's death:

> It is said, by parties who claim their ability to sustain it, that the reward of $1000 dollars, offered by the Stockraiser's Protective Association for Curly Bill, was claimed by Wyatt Earp, and the amount in horses and money, paid to him by H.C. Hooker last Monday. Possibly this is true; but it is rough on the party who paid the reward, as the notorious and wily William is beyond question of doubt alive in New Mexico, keeping his weather eye open for a fresh saddle horse. Any how it was a neat job.

Another reason for Wyatt to make a false claim may have been to regain the public's trust and popular support by deflecting attention from the Earp party's misdeeds and focusing the people's concentration elsewhere. At least that was the overall effect that the "Wyatt Earp killed Curly Bill" story had, whether intentional or not, on the people throughout the territory. Rather than continuing to publish articles about how the Earp party were fugitives who had murdered Frank Stilwell and Florentino Cruz, the newspapers, instead, started bickering about whether Wyatt had really killed Curly Bill Brocius. On April 1, 1882, the *Tombstone Nugget* made this offer to its readers: "The reward offered for Curly Bill was $1000. The same was, we have good reason to believe, paid to Wyatt Earp upon false representations. The NUGGET has said that Curly William is alive. If any one will produce any evidence, affidavits or otherwise, that he is not, we will produce $1,000 in fifteen minutes and present the same to them." Later the *Epitaph* countered with its own proposal: "If Curly Bill will present himself, thereby proving himself alive, we will donate the sum of $2000 to any deserving charity he may mention—the Stock-raisers' Protective Association, for instance." Neither reward was claimed.[23]

Some writers have argued that the notorious cowboy's sudden disappearance from Arizona and the fact that he never show up again anywhere are strong evidence that Wyatt Earp killed him.[24] Yet, old-timers maintained that Curly had left Arizona long before the battle at the spring.[25] In actuality, Curly did not "suddenly vanish" from Arizona—he was rumored to have already left Arizona and one report even claimed he died a month before the fight at the spring.[26] Only a few unsubstantiated rumors even place the cowboy in Arizona after December 1881, and no documented evidence has ever been presented that he was still in the territory at the time of the clash in the Whetstone Mountains.[27] If the cowboy had already left Arizona for parts unknown, it is reasonable and understandable he did not immediately surface in Arizona to refute the claim that Wyatt killed him. While news of the incident provably spread throughout the country, there were also many remote areas throughout the West and Mexico that likely did not receive the news of the battle for weeks or even months, if ever.[28] Still, there are stories of Curly Bill returning to Arizona after Wyatt Earp left the territory. William Breakenridge later recalled two accounts of Curly Bill returning to Arizona:

> A reliable merchant and rancher living at Safford told me that about two weeks after the Earp party reported killing Curly Bill, Curly himself came to his home and said he just got back from Old Mexico; that he was leaving the country and going to Wyoming where he was going to get work and try to lead a decent life, as he was tired of being on the dodge all the time. The merchant gave him a good saddle horse to ride away

on. A Mr. Vaughn, now living in Tombstone, told me that ten years later Curly Bill came through Benson on the train bound for Texas, and stopped off long enough to vist the postmaster, whom he had known in his earlier days in Arizona.[29]

Of course, neither of the uncorroborated hearsay statements presented by Breakenridge, offers any real proof of the cowboy's appearance in Arizona after the shootout at Mescal Springs. However, Wyatt Earp's claim is not supported by any real proof either.

Other accounts place a man named Curly Bill roaming around the Arizona-New Mexico area as late as 1886. For example, the *Silver City Enterprise,* on March 26, 1886, commented: "John Coughan, a would-be bad man, and another rather notorious character who delights in the sobriquet of 'Curly Bill,' came into the city Tuesday evening, and forthwith proceeded to paint the town." The following morning Coughan tried to shoot a Mexican in a saloon but hit a bystander in the left arm. "After the shooting, Coughan and Curly got their horses and left the city."[30] There's no proof that this man was William Brocius of Tombstone fame, and there were other men in the West that used the name Curly Bill, but the possibility remains that it was the notorious cowboy.

An article published by the *National Police Gazette* on January 23, 1882, suggests that the cowboy may have gone to Colorado prior to the "Battle at Burleigh Springs." This national publication printed a picture of William A. Rogers, also known as Curly Bill, the city marshal of St. Elmo, Colorado, who was "known to have killed at least seven men in Colorado, Arizona and Montana."[31] Interestingly, a man named "Rogers, or Curly Bill" had been reported shot at San Simon during August 1880.[32] Was this man Curly Bill Brocius? There is no way at this point to confirm that they were the same man. Yet, the presence of a "Curly Bill Rogers" in San Simon at roughly the same time as Brocius, remains an intriguing coincidence at the very least.

Montana is another location sometimes cited as Curly Bill's residence after leaving Arizona. Old-timer Melvin Jones, steadfastly and without corroboration, claimed that Curly Bill, whose real name was "William Graham," had gone to Montana.[33] In response, old-timer James C. Hancock, disputed Jones' claim by asserting that William Graham and William Brocius were two different men.[34] Hancock further maintained that Jim Hughes, an associate and friend of Curly Bill, years later told him that Curly Bill was in New Mexico when Wyatt said he killed Brocius.[35] There is very little evidence available, however, to substantiate either man's account.

Some contemporary reports suggesting another possibility for the notorious cowboy's whereabouts nonetheless have survived. Shortly after he was supposedly killed, a "reliable" man came to Silver City, New Mexico, and categorically told the newspaper editor there that "Curly Bill is not dead." [36] Yet, the editor had his doubts about the report and in response to the claim sarcastically wrote: "The reported death of Jesse James is also denied."[37] Other "sightings" of Curly Bill nevertheless reached newspaper editors in the West. On June 26, 1883, the *El Paso Daily Times* wrote, "'Curly Bill,' so often reported killed, is in Old Mexico," but so is "'Johnny Over-the-fence'; two or three other Bills and in the words of the concert-hall poet, 'the rest of the gang'." Three weeks later, on July 14, 1883, the *Weekly Arizona Citizen* (Tucson) proclaimed that Curly Bill was in Chihuahua, Mexico:

Arizona News

Curley Bill, a cow-boy, who obtained an unenviable notoriety in Tombstone a couple of years ago, and has been reported killed several times since, is said to have discovered, in connection with another party, some very rich silver mines in Chihuahua.[Clifton Clarion]

Did Curly Bill leave Arizona and eventually settle in Chihuahua, Mexico? That Mexican state was experiencing a mining boom similar to the one that happened in Tombstone, and much of the same problems that affected Arizona were now occuring in Chihuahua. Americans flooded the region looking to make money from mining and the associated business that surrounded it. Of course, cowboys of the same ilk as Curly Bill arrived on the scene to torment the local inhabitants and wreaked havoc as they did in Arizona. For example, Pony Deal, an outlaw and desperado well-known in Tombstone, came to Chihuahua after leaving Arizona but was extradited by Mexican officials to New Mexico in 1884.[38]

The "Curly Bill is alive and well, and living in Chihuahua" story, which had it beginnings by 1883, took root and spread over the next forty years. In Allen Erwin's 1965 biography of John Slaughter, sheriff of Cochise County in the late 1880s, an outlaw from Mexico named Eduardo Moreno is described as being an in-law of Curly Bill— supposedly Curly married one of Moreno's female relatives upon arriving in Mexico.[39] Nineteen years after the *El Paso Daily Times* noted that Curly Bill was in Mexico[40] and the *Arizona Weekly Citizen* commented that Curly Bill was living at Chihuahua[41], the *Clifton Copper Era*, on January 9, 1902, maintained that the cowboy had "quit his funny business, had married and settled down in the State of Chihuahua, Mexico." Writer Grace McCool, a folklorist who repeated old-timer claims, later wrote, without support, that a man named Avery Curry had visited Curly Bill in Chihuahua, where the "former outlaw" was a "prosperous rancher."[42] According to Curry's story, "Curly left Arizona, as the Benson postmaster had claimed, but Wyoming was so torn by the cattle wars that Curly traveled down to Chihuahua."[43] Other old-timers like J. C. Hancock, also wrote that Curly Bill lived out his life in Mexico, but none of these accounts are definitive.[44] Of course, tracking a drifter such as Curly Bill, a man of many aliases whose true name is uncertain and whose origins continue to elude researchers, isn't easy.

Over the years, Wyatt Earp continued to claim that he had killed Curly Bill in the Whetstone Mountains, and the story got better each time it was told. One of the first to hear Wyatt's account was Ed Colburn, a Dodge City lawyer visiting Gunnison, Colorado. Colburn wrote a letter to the *Ford County Globe* detailing his conversation with Wyatt Earp, and the newspaper published it on May 23, 1882:

LETTER FROM E. F. COLBURN.

Gunnison, Col., May 20, 1882

Editor Globe:

Wyatt and Warren Earp arrived here some days ago and will remain awhile. Wyatt is more robust than when a resident of Dodge, but in other respects is unchanged. His story of a long contest with the cow boys of Arizona is of absorbing interest. Of five brothers four yet live, and in return for the assasination of Morgan Earp they have handed seven cow boys "over to the majority."

Of the six who actually participated in the assasination they have killed three—among them, Curly Bill, whom Wyatt believes killed Mike Mayer [Meager], at Caldwell, last summer. [Frank] Stillwell, Curly Bill and party ambuscaded the Earp party and poured a deadly fire into them, Wyatt receiving a charge of buckshot through his overcoat on each side of his body and having the horn of his saddle shot off. Wyatt says after the first shock he could distinguish Dave Rudebaugh and Curly Bill, the latter's body showing well among the bushes. Wyatt lost no time in taking him in, and will receive the $1,000 offered. From what I could learn, the Earps have killed all, or nearly all of the leaders of the element of cow boys, who number in all about 150, and the troubles in Arizona will, so far as they are concerned, be over.

Wyatt expects to become a candidate for sheriff of Cochise County this fall, and as he stands

very near the Governor and all the good citizens of
Tombstone and other camps in Cochise County he
will without doubt be elected. The office is said to be
worth $25,000 per annum and will not be bad to take.

There is no record of Dave Rudabaugh, an outlaw well known
in Kansas, New Mexico, and Texas, even being in Arizona. Moreover,
Curly Bill had nothing at all to do with the death of Mike Meagher
(Wyatt's former boss in Wichita) in Caldwell, Kansas, on December
17, 1881.[45] Obviously, Wyatt added details to the account that were
familiar to Colburn in order to impress him—showing Wyatt's tendency
to doctor stories to credulous audiences as early as 1882.

Eleven years later, in 1893, Wyatt Earp was interviewed in
Colorado about the battle at the spring. Curly Bill "churned several
shots at me with his Winchester" rifle, "but he fired rapidly and his
bullets went wild," recalled Wyatt.[46] "I threw my shotgun to my
shoulder and fixing a bead directly on his heart, turned loose both
barrels. His chest was torn open by the big charge of buckshot. He
yelled like a demon when he went down."[47] Wyatt Earp pulled out
all the stops in storytelling three years later by spinning an impressive
tale in a series of three articles published by the *San Francisco
Examiner*.[48] In one article, Earp stated that Curly Bill was "trying to
pump some lead into me with a Winchester" rifle.[49] "I fired both
barrels of my gun into him, blowing him all to pieces," Earp recalled.[50]
A week later, on August 9, 1896, while he was discussing "tales of
the shotgun messenger service," Wyatt changed his story about the
weapon Curly Bill used during the fight: "Toward the end of my story
last Sunday I described the killing of Curly Bill. By an inadvertency I
said that he opened up on me with a Winchester. I should have said a
Wells-Fargo shotgun."[51] Wyatt then asserted that Curly Bill had taken
the Wells, Fargo shotgun from Charles Bartholomew during a stage
robbery on January 6, 1882.[52]

Despite Wyatt's tale, Curly Bill was not implicated in the
robbery at the time.[53] More importantly, the shotgun, which was for a
short time believed to have been stolen during the holdup, was

solemnly spoke of them as flowers that the real artist might paint with rapture the audience became grim and rigid again. At the finish of the lecture the poet was vigorously applauded, and when he retired from the stage he blushed like a school-girl.

"Curly Bill," of Colorado.

W. A. Rogers, alias "Curly Bill," City Marshal of St. Elmo, Col., and a candidate for sheriff of Chaffee county at the recent eléction, is one of the most notorious and desperate characters in the west; he is known to have killed at least seven men in Colorado, Arizona and Montana, and his official career has been little less bloody than that of the great stage robbers, "Billy the Kid" and Simmons, the latter once being a partner of "Curly Bill's." Rogers is never known to smile except when in the act of taking the life of a fellow creature; he will doubtless soon file another

William A. Rogers, "Curly Bill of Colorado." Was he the Curly Bill Brocius? National Police Gazette, January 23, 1882.

W. A. ROGERS,

ALIAS "CURLY BILL," CITY MARSHAL OF ST. ELMO, COL., THE HERO OF NUMEROUS RENCONTRES AND SHOOTING SCRAPES IN THE WILD WEST.

notch in his pistol barrel as he has been challenged by J. S. Painter, editor of the *South Arkansas Miner*, of Maysville, Col., to fight a duel to the death. The weapons to be used are pistols, and in the event of neither being killed by those weapons the duel is to be continued with knives. Painter is little less noted as a "bad man" than his opponent though the notches on his pistol are not so numerous as are those on the gun of Rogers'.

Painter's career will doubtless end with the coming duel as "Curly Bill" is a dead shot, as he has frequently, in the streets of St. Elmo, given exhibitions of his skill by taking a pistol in each hand and putting two bullet holes into a tin can, thrown into the air, before it reached the ground. The boys of St. Elmo are on the *qui vive* for the coming event, hoping to give Painter a grand send off to the happy hunting grounds, as Rogers, who is a great favorite of the boys, says he'll "plug" him sure. Rogers began his career as an officer at Maroa, Ill., having acted as a policeman there.

discovered by a Mexican in the desert near the road where the robbery took place prior to the battle at the spring. The *Tombstone Nugget*, on March 14, 1882, published the following story:

> That Missing Shotgun
> At the time the Bisbee stage was robbed, the messenger, Charles Bartholomew, was armed with a short double-barreled shotgun, a Winchester rifle, and possibly a revolver or two. After the fight was over and the treasure gone, the shotgun was also missing, and the messenger entertained an opinion that it had been taken by the highwaymen, but subsequent events prove that it was in all probability dropped during the melee. Last Saturday Deputy Sheriff Frank Hereford, while on his way to Charleston, met a Mexican carrying a gun, which he immediately recognized as the property of Wells, Fargo & Co. The man was arrested, and explained that he had traded a pistol to his cousin for the gun, which was found near the place where the coach had been robbed, and, singular as it may seem, both barrels were loaded when it was picked up. One side of the barrels being rusty served to confirm the Mexican's statement that it had lain for some time on the ground exposed to the elements. Should it again escape, it will be arrested and punished under the provisions of the vagrant act.

Wyatt Earp never stopped telling the "I Killed Curly Bill who was armed with Bartholomew's Wells, Fargo shotgun" story to those interested in his adventures. In *Wyatt Earp, Frontier Marshal*, Stuart Lake repeated a particularly elaborate version of the tale, which included this comment attributed to Earp about the lost-and-found weapon: "I saw the Wells-Fargo plate on the gun Curly Bill was using . . . ."[54] Why would a man present a story that is patently false if the event he was describing really happened? Once it is shown that Wyatt Earp doctored his story of the killing of Curly Bill, how can one accept the rest of it without contemporary, independent confirmation? And that is the fundamental problem with accepting Wyatt's word that he killed Curly Bill Brocius—there is no contemporary, independent confirmation that he killed the notorious cowboy.

Other people who lived in Tombstone at the time the shooting occurred also wrote about the event. One was William Breakenridge, who asserted that two of the men at the spring were Alex Arnold and Pink Truly, and that they told the following story to a man in Tombstone:

> They said that Curly Bill was not there; that he had been in Mexico for the past two months. As the Earp party rode up to the spring the cowboys took refuge behind an embankment, and all but Wyatt of the Earp party turned and rode away. Wyatt, however, rode up rather close to them and dismounted, and with the bridle rein over his arm stepped in front of his horse, raised his rifle and fired at them. They returned fire. Alex Arnold reported that Earp was wearing a white shirt which made a splendid target. He was only a short distance away and drew a fine bead on Wyatt and fired. Earp turned partly around and staggered back toward his horse which he mounted and rode away after the other of his party. Both Truly and Arnold claimed that Wyatt Earp had a steel vest on under his shirt which deflected the bullet.[55]

Of course, there is no way to confirm the statements told to Breakenridge years later, nevertheless, there were reports at the time that Wyatt was believed to have been shot during the encounter. Following the fight at the spring, Deputy Sheriff Frank Hereford returned to Tombstone after a tax assessing trip down the San Pedro River and he reportedly corroborated the story that Wyatt was injured at the spring. Hereford claimed that he had gone to a house "north of Willcox, and while there saw a body of horsemen coming from the south. Not knowing who they were, he stepped into a side room, and awaited there arrival."[56] The deputy "who could plainly overhear all that was said, soon discovered that his immediate neighbors were none other than the Earp party."[57] Hereford wanted to avoid a possible fight with the men, so he stayed in the side room until the Earp party had left the house. The *Arizona Weekly Star* later noted, "The sheriff's officer with his shotgun at a 'ready' was an interested listener. It seems that Texas Jack had his horse killed by the first volley and that Wyatt Earp received a couple of ugly flesh wounds in the region of the breast and shoulders."[58] Deputy Hereford's account made its way to Tucson, and according to an account in the *Arizona Weekly Star*, Hereford claimed to have witnessed the shootout at the spring:

> The deputy sheriff above referred to states that four prospectors were encamped temporarily in the canyon and in the act of preparing their noon meal, when a shower of lead in their midst naturally attracted their attention and a like compliment in return. The prospectors when the first shock was over, grasped their guns, and glancing in the direction of their assailants were surprised to see, instead of a party of Apaches as they expected, eight white men on horseback blazing away as fast as Winchesters could pump lead.[59]

The newspaper article stated that "the Earp party attacked a party of propsectors on that occasion, instead of cowboys as reported." When the fight occurred, "the prospectors, who were under the lead of a party named Dan Murphy, turned their shotguns loose, and the so-called defenders of the law and order beat a retreat."[60]

Fred Dodge, was another man who later claimed he was told about the details of the incident by an alleged participant. According to Dodge, who claimed to have been a secret Wells, Fargo agent in Tombstone, Johnny Barnes was wounded in the encounter and later died of his wound. However, before his death, Barnes told Dodge that "Wyatt throwed down on Curly Bill right across his horse and killed him."[61] Many writers have accepted Dodge's assertion at face value over the years—using his allegation that Barnes told him that Curly Bill was killed at the spring to substantiate Wyatt's claim—but Dodge's trustworthiness has been questioned recently.[62]

Nonetheless, for many people, then and now, the saga of Curly Bill Brocius ended with Wyatt Earp's shotgun blast at Mescal Springs. After all, Earp was an eyewitness and a participant in the shootout. Furthermore, Wyatt on several occasions over the remainder of his life asserted that he killed Curly Bill.

Well, did Wyatt Earp kill Curly Bill Brocius? This writer believes he did not. Considering that Wyatt had a penchant for doctoring the story and that he provided the sole basis for the claim, it is difficult to accept his word on the matter.[63] Even if Earp did not make up the story to collect a reward or to gain popular support, one must consider that during the melee at the spring, Wyatt was firing and fleeing at the same time, making it almost impossible for him to know the results of his shots. He didn't walk up to a dead victim, roll the body over, and confirm that the man was Curly Bill. It would have been difficult for Wyatt to identify his adversary from a distance of thirty yards during the heat of battle. Wyatt may have believed that Curly Bill was there and may have believed he shot the cowboy, but he couldn't have known for sure.

In simple terms, the evidence that Curly Bill left Arizona before March 1882 is stronger than the evidence that he was killed by Wyatt at a spring in the Whetstone Mountains. There are simply too many reports pointing to Chihuahua as Curly's eventual place of residence after leaving Arizona to dismiss out of hand the possibility that the notorious cowboy lived for many years in that Mexican state.

Nonetheless, because no definitive evidence is available establishing what really happened that day in March 1882, Wyatt Earp's claim that he killed Curly Bill Brocius will continue to spark heated debate and controversy. In a way, the headlines of one article in the *Tombstone Epitaph* was prophetic:

BATTLE OF BURLEIGH

Two Versions of the Fight.

**You Pays Your Money and You
Takes Your Choice.** [64]

The author's money is on Curly Bill Brocius surviving the "Battle of Burleigh Springs." [65]

APPENDIX

COURT DOCUMENTS

A subpoena was issued to summon the appearance of Francis Fowden, George Blond, Henry Raymond, and John Woods to testify in Curly Bill and Bob Martin's criminal case. Case 300—Robert Martin et al, El Paso Count Clerk's Office, El Paso, Texas.

Appeal filed by Curly Bill and Bob Martin seeking a new trial after their conviction in Texas. Case 300—Robert Martin et al, El Paso Count Clerk's Office, El Paso, Texas.

Prosecutor's response to the appeal filed by Curly Bill and Bob Martin seeking a new trial after their conviction in Texas. Case 300—Robert Martin et al, El Paso Count Clerk's Office, El Paso, Texas.

Indictment found against Curly Bill and Bob Martin in El Paso County, El Paso, Texas. Case 300—Robert Martin et al, El Paso Count Clerk's Office, El Paso, Texas.

Notes and Sources

Chapter One. ALIAS CURLY BILL

1. *Tombstone Epitaph*, October 28, 1880.
2. Ibid.
3. *Tucson Daily Citizen*, December 27, 1880.
4. Ibid.
5. *Tucson Daily Citizen*, December 27, 1880; *Tombstone Epitaph*, November 1, 1880.
6. *Tucson Daily Citizen*, December 27, 1880.
7. *Arizona Daily Star*, July 18, 1882.
8. *Tombstone Epitaph*, October 29, 1880.
9. Cause 300, State of Texas v Robert Martin and William Bresnaham. El Paso County District Court Clerk's Office, El Paso, Texas.
10. The *Tombstone Epitaph*'s initial news story about the shooting of Fred White did not identify Curly Bill by name or by his moniker. The next day, on October 29, 1880, the *Tombstone Epitaph* commented that "he gave his name as William Rosciotis [sic] and claimed to hail from San Simon country." On October 31, 1880, the *Tombstone Epitaph* referred to White's assailant as Byoscins [sic] and Broscins [sic]. Thus, it is clear that "Curly Bill Brocius" was not a well-known figure in Tombstone at the time Fred White was shot.
11. Cause 300, State of Texas v Robert Martin and William Bresnaham. El Paso County District Court Clerk's Office, El Paso, Texas.
12. Reminiscences of Melvin Jones. Arizona Historical Society Library, Tucson, Arizona. Jones claimed that Curly Bill came to Arizona working a cattle drive during November 1878, and that he was told that

the cowboy was dubbed with the nickname Curly Bill by a saloon girl on the trip: "Frank [Brigham] began, We went one night to a saloon dance house and a woman sang nice songs to us with the part of the chorus going 'My fair haired Billie boy.' Bill Graham had been dancing with a spanish girl that could not talk much English. After the dance, the singing woman put her hands on Bill's head and sang: 'He's my curley headed Billie boy.' That made the spanish girl mad, she flared up and said: 'You lie, He my Curley Bill boy.' Then the two women started fighting. That I am sure is the beginning of the name Curley Bill for Bill Graham. Bill's brother, George, was with him on this drive from Texas. But when Bill had to go on trial for the killing of Marshal White in Tombstone, he gave the name of William Brocius." Since Curly escaped from the Texas Rangers on November 2, 1878, it's plausible that he could have joined a cattle drive and been in Arizona in late November. However, Curly Bill could not have earned his sobriquet during a November 1878 cattle drive—he was already using the nickname six months earlier when he was arrested on May 22, 1878. Other than Melvin Jones' assertion, no supporting contemporary evidence that Curly Bill was named William Graham has been found.

13. Ibid.

14. Reminiscences of J.C. Hancock. Arizona Historical Society Library, Tucson, Arizona. According to Hancock, "Curly Bill wore his hair quite long and it was very curly. He was always playing the French harp. The rustlers had a camp in some boulders south of Paradise and it was kept by an old rounder named Scotty. The way the rustlers made their money was to go into Mexico and steal horses and cattle and bring them up here to Arizona where they could sell them at a good price. Once when the Mexicans went after the gang, Curly Bill got separated from the rest and the Mexicans shot him in the butt, but did not hit a bone. Bill rode over 200 miles to Lordsburg to see a doctor." Like Melvin Jones' reminiscences, Hancock's stories can neither be proved nor refuted.

15. Ibid.

16. Burns, Walter Noble, *Tombstone, An Iliad of the Southwest* (New York: Doubleday, 1927) p.78; Lake, Stuart N., *Wyatt Earp, Frontier Marshal* (New York: Houghton Mifflin, 1931), pp. 234-235. "Curly Bill, who gave his name as William Brocius, as appears by the official records, though old-timers who knew him say it [his name] was

William Graham," wrote Burns. Lake stated that Curly Bill Brocius "sometimes gave his name as Graham." In contrast, William Breakenridge, who was a deputy sheriff at Tombstone, in his book *Helldorado: Bringing the Law to the Mesquite* (Boston: Houghton-Mifflin, 1928), made no reference to Curly Bill being known by the name Graham at all.

17. Nolan, Frederick, *The Lincoln County War: A Documentary History* (Norman: University of Oklahoma Press, 1992).

18. Anonymous letter from the Brocius family found in Phil Rasch Collection, MS 677, Box 1, File 1, Arizona Historical Society, Tucson, Arizona. The letter was published in Bill Kelly's *Encyclopedia of Gunfighters*.

19. Letter from Glenn Mears to Ben Traywick. Courtesy Ben Traywick.

20. No trace of a William Brocius was found in the land records of Crawfordsville. There was a Mary M. Brosius who had married a man named Christopher Dice in 1869, but not a Charles Comer as the account claimed (Montgomery County Marriage Records, 1860-1920). They were married on February 11, 1869 (*A History of "Union" Presbyterian Church, Walnut Township, Montgomery County, Indiana, 1834-1939*, compiled by W. Arthur Porter, pg. 43). Therefore, a ring of plausibility does exist in the account, but it contains no real proof. In the 1870 Indiana census, there is a William listed as a son of Christopher Dice. Yet, it appears that his full name was William A. Dice (not Brosius) and he lived in Indiana a number of years—marrying at least two women in the area during his life (*Montgomery County, Indiana, Will and Marriage Records, Vol. III* by Mable V. Shanklin). However, what makes this particular claim intriguing is that in the 1860 federal census for Indiana there were also two women named Bresnaham in the Crawfordsville area. A search of the nearby counties did produce a William H. Brosius (a letter written to Curly Bill during 1881 identified his name as William H. Brosius) in Henry County—information on this William Brosius is hard to find. However, land and census records indicate that a man named William M. Brosius, who also had a son named William, were in the area prior to the Civil War. William Brosius served in the Union army from September 16, 1861, to June 20, 1862. He received a disability discharge. The following year, a William Brosius was listed has having been in state service as part of

the Morgan Raid Minutemen from July 12 to July 18, 1863 (*Hazzard's History of Henry County*). Two years later a William Brosius and William Leonard were paid $2.00 apiece for serving as marshals on the 29th and 30th of July 1865. William M. Brosius Sr. died on February 25, 1873, and his son, William M. Brosius Jr. died eight months later, on October 27, 1873. The son was buried in the Old Knightstown Cemetery. It seems unlikely that the Brosius family would have a burial ceremony without the body eight years after the Civil War was over. Of course, if there is no body in the grave then the basic story would be plausible—but there still would be no proof directly linking Curly Bill Brocius with this man. It seems more likely that a relative named William H. Brosius, possibly an uncle or cousin to William M. Brosius Jr., lived in the area. Thus, he would be a better candidate for possibly being Curly Bill Brocius.

21. Ibid.

22. Brosius, Lewis Walton, *Geneology of Henry and Mary Brosius and their Descendents* (Wilmington: Self-Published, 1928).

23. Artrip, Louise and Fullen, *Memoirs of Late Daniel Fore (Jim) Chisholm And The Chisholm Trail* (Booneville: Artrip Publications, 1959).

24. Artrip, Louise and Fullen, *Memoirs of Late Daniel Fore (Jim) Chisholm And The Chisholm Trail* (Booneville: Artrip Publications, 1959). Ten years earlier, however, the Artrips published *Memoirs of Daniel Fore (Jim) Chisholm And The Chisholm Trail* (Booneville: Artrip Publications, 1949), which does not contain the later account that Curly Bill's name was William Brocius Graham. Thus, we are left with another claim that is not corroborated by any evidence.

25. *Phoenix Herald*, May 27, 1881. It is possible that Curly Bill may have been from Texas or may have lived for some time. An 1878 Fugitives From Justice report for Texas listed, "Brusues, Wm; alias Bill Burns," who was wanted on two separate indictments filed on January 3, 1873, in McLennon County, Texas, for the theft of bales of cotton. (Letter from Dave Johnson dated August 23, 1984). Although there was William Burns in McLennen County that was born around 1859, he is listed in the 1880 Federal Census for Texas. Thus, it seems unlikly he could have been Curly Bill. A William Albert Brosius was born in Lamar, Texas, on September 1, 1858, and married Annie Ewbank at Paris, Texas on December 20, 1883. However, there is no proof that he was Curly Bill.

26. Breakenridge, William, *Helldorado: Bringing the Law to the Mesquite,* p. 130.

27. Phil Rasch Collection, MS 677, Box 1, File 1, Arizona Historical Society, Tucson, Arizona. A man wrote a letter to Rasch claiming that Brocius was part African-American. Although there is no proof that this was the case, there were Brocius families in Texas that were black.

28. While a few photographs purportedly of Curly Bill have surfaced, the provenance for these pictures is questionable.

29. Cause 300, State of Texas v Robert Martin and William Bresnaham. El Paso County District Court Clerk's Office, El Paso, Texas.

30. Bailey, Lynn R., ed., *A Tenderfoot in Tombstone: The Private Journal of George Whitwell Parsons - The Turbulent Years, 1880 - 1882,* p. 182.

31. *Tucson Daily Citizen,* December 27, 1880.

32. *Arizona Weekly Citizen,* January 22, 1881.

33. Bailey, Lynn R., ed., *A Tenderfoot in Tombstone: The Private Journal of George Whitwell Parsons - The Turbulent Years, 1880 - 1882,* p. 118; *Arizona Daily Star,* on January 27, 1881.

34. Ibid.

35. *Arizona Weekly Star,* on May 26, 1881.

Chapter Two. ON THE ROAD TO MESILLA

1. As Spanish explorers approached the Rio Grande River from the south in 1581, they viewed two mountain ranges with a deep chasm between them. They named the site "El Paso Del Norte" (the Pass of the North). Following the Treaty of Guadalupe Hidalgo in 1847, the Rio Grande River became the border between the United States and Mexico, and El Paso Del Norte became a border town. By 1849, five settlements were founded by Anglo-Americans on the north side of the border. One was named Franklin, but pioneer "Anson Mills named this settlement El Paso, thus generating considerable confusion that lasted for almost thirty years." El Paso Del Norte was renamed Ciudad Juarez on September 16, 1888. Handbook of Texas Online: *El Paso Del Norte,* The Texas State Historical Association. See also Sonnichsen, C. L., *Pass of the North: Four Centuries on the Rio Grande* (El Paso: Texas Western Press, 1968); Timmons, W. H., *El Paso: A Borderlands*

History (El Paso: Texas Western Press, 1990).

2. J. A. Tays to John B. Jones, letter dated May 16, 1878. Adjutant General Records, Letters Received, Texas State Library and Archives, Austin, Texas.

3. *Mesilla Valley Independent*, May 23, 1878.

4. *Mesilla Valley Independent*, May 23, 1878. See also Gatto, Steve, *Alias Curly Bill, The Life and Times of William Brocius* (Tucson: Privately printed, 2000) p. 5.

5. *Mesilla Valley Independent*, June 1, 1878.

6. J. A. Tays to John B. Jones, letter dated November 6, 1878. Adjutant General Records, Letters Received, Texas State Library and Archives, Austin, Texas. Tays made the following comment in his letter: "We have to chain the prisoners in the yard to stakes at night and in the day if warm let them remain round the yard and when the weather is cold they are put in the room and it being a long dark room without any windows." See also Brand, Peter, "The Escape of 'Curly Bill' Brocius," Western Outlaw Lawman Association *Quarterly*, Summer 2000.

7. J. A. Tays to John B. Jones, letter dated May 31, 1878. Adjutant General Records, Letters Received, Texas State Library and Archives, Austin, Texas.

8. Nolan, Fred, "Boss Rustler: The Life and Crimes of John Kinney, Part 1." *True West*, Vol. 43, No. 9, September 1996, p. 18.

9. Handbook of Texas Online: *El Paso* and *Salt War of San Elizario*, The Texas State Historical Association. See also Sonnichsen, C. L., *The El Paso Salt War* (El Paso: Hertzog, 1961).

10. Ibid.

11. Nolan, Fred, "Boss Rustler: The Life and Crimes of John Kinney, Part 1." *True West*, Vol. 43, No. 9, September 1996, p. 18.

12. Ibid.

13. Handbook of Texas Online: *El Paso* and *Salt War of San Elizario*, The Texas State Historical Association. See also Sonnichsen, C. L., *The El Paso Salt War* (El Paso: Hertzog, 1961).

14. Dona Ana County Criminal Record F, 1875-1878, New Mexico State Archives, Sante Fe, New Mexico. Bob Martin and Ruperto Lara were indicted by the Dona Ana County grand jury for stealing cattle on June 28, 1877. Jesus Valancia was also charged with the crime. On November 17, 1878, the case was stricken from the court docket with leave to reinstate the case.

15. *Mesilla Valley Independent*, June 1, 1878.

16. Monthly Return of Company C, Frontier Forces, State of Texas, dated September 30, 1878, Texas State Library and Archives, Austin, Texas.

17. *Mesilla Valley Independent*, September 6, 1878.

18. Cause 300, State of Texas v Robert Martin and William Bresnaham. El Paso County District Court Clerk's Office, El Paso, Texas.

19. Gatto, Steve, *Alias Curly Bill, The Life and Times of William Brocius* (Tucson: Privately printed, 2000), pp. 6-8. See also Gatto, Steve, *Wyatt Earp, A Biography of a Western Lawman* (Tucson: San Simon Publishing, 1997), pp. 65-66; Gatto, Steve, *Real Wyatt Earp* (Silver City: High-Lonesome Press, 2000), p. 49.

20. *Denver Tribune*, May 17, 1882.

21. Boatner, Mark, *The Civil War Dictionary* (Vintage Books, Reprint Edition, 1999).

22. Cause 300, State of Texas vs. Robert Martin and William Bresnaham. El Paso County District Court Clerk's Office, El Paso, Texas.

23. Ibid.

24. Ibid.

25. Ibid.

26. Ibid.

27. Ibid.

28. Monthly Return of Company C, Frontier Forces, State of Texas, dated September 30, 1878, Texas State Library and Archives, Austin, Texas.

29. J. A. Tays to John B. Jones, letter dated September 30, 1878. Adjutant General Records, Letters Received, Texas State Library and Archives, Austin, Texas.

30. J. A. Tays to John B. Jones, letter dated November 6, 1878. Adjutant General Records, Letters Received, Texas State Library and Archives, Austin, Texas.

31. Ibid.

32. Bryan Callaghan to John B. Jones, letter dated December 9, 1878. Adjutant General Records, Letters Received, Texas State Library and Archives, Austin, Texas.

Chapter Three. ROBERT MARTIN GANG

1. Cool, Paul, "Bob Martin: A Rustler in Paradise," Western Outlaw Lawman Association *Quarterly*, Winter 2003.
2. Ibid.
3. Letter from Department of State to Carl Schurz, Secretary of the Interior, dated December 10, 1878, which transcribed a letter written by the Mexican Minister on December 6, 1878. Cowboy Depredations File, U.S. Document [microfilm], Record Group 60, University of Arizona Library, Tucson, Arizona.
4. Rasch, Phil, "The Resurrection of Pony Deal," Phil Rasch Collection, Arizona Historical Society Library, Tucson, Arizona
5. J. A. Tays to John B. Jones, letter dated November 6, 1878. Adjutant General Records, Letters Received, Texas State Library and Archives, Austin, Texas. Brand, Peter, "The Escape of 'Curly Bill' Brocius."
6. *Tombstone Daily Epitaph*, July 30, 1880.
7. Lake, *Wyatt Earp, Frontier Marshal,* p. 240.
8. 1880 New Mexico Federal Census, Grant County, New Mexico.
9. The *Tombstone Epitaph*, on October 23, 1881, reported that deputy William Breakenridge had arrested Milt Hicks, "who is charged with having in his possession and fraudulently branding cattle belonging to a rancher." On the afternoon of October 24, Hicks and two other prisoners overpowered their guard and escaped from the county jail. On October 25, 1881, the *Tombstone Epitaph* noted the escape and that "Sheriff Behan, Deputies Breakenridge, [Andy] Bronk and [Lance] Perkins, Chief of Police Earp, Morgan Earp, Wyatt Earp and several others started in pursuit" but could not find the escaped men. Milt Hicks fled to New Mexico, joining his brother Will, who had already crossed over to New Mexico to avoid arrest.
10. Hill, Janaloo, *Yours Until Death, William Grounds, True West,* April 1973, p. 14.
11. Register of Complaints, Cochise County Court Clerk's Office, Bisbee, Arizona. Like Milt and Will Hicks, Led Moore fled to New Mexico. He was never arrested on the criminal charge.
12. 1880 New Mexico Federal Census, Grant County, New Mexico.
13. *Arizona Weekly Star*, November 10, 1881.

14. Gatto, Steve, *Johnny Ringo* (Lansing: Protar House, 2002). See Also Johnson, David, *John Ringo* (Stillwater: Barbed Wire Press, 1996).

15. Gatto, Steve, *The Real Wyatt Earp* (Silver City: High-Lonesome Books, 2000), p. 84. See Also Carmony, Neil B., ed., *Apache Days and Tombstone Nights: John Clum's Autobiography* (Silver City: High-Lonesome Books, 1997), pp. 4-10, 54, 56.

16. The *Tombstone Daily Epitaph,* on August 6, 1880, noted Ike Clanton's arrival from San Simon with "fifty head of beef cattle for the Tombstone market."

17. New Mexico Land Records. Grant County District Court Clerk's Office, Silver City, New Mexico; Gatto Steve, "Johnny Ringo, Land and Cattle Speculator," National Outlaw Lawman Association *Quarterly* Vol.18, No. 4, 1994, pp. 9-10.

18. Cool, Paul, "Bob Martin: A Rustler in Paradise," p. 28, citing a letter from Walz to Loud, January 22, 1879 (NA Microfilm M1088, Roll 209).

19. Cool, Paul, "Bob Martin: A Rustler in Paradise," pp. 28-29, citing Senor Rueles, Minister of Foreign Affairs to Mr. John W. Foster, Minister of USA to Mexico, April 22, 1879.

20. Ibid.

21. *Thirty-Four* (Las Cruces), September 3, 1879; Cool, Paul, "Bob Martin: A Rustler in Paridise," p. 29, citing Baylor to Jones, November 20, 1880, Texas State Library Archives Commission ("TSLAC").

22. Cool, Paul, "Bob Martin: A Rustler in Paradise," pp. 33-34. About the function of "middlemen"in the process, Cool commented: "Across the border, middlemen . . . found ranchers looking to build herds or contractors buying for the U.S. Government." Cool noted that contractor Benjamin Schuster was found with stolen cattle from "Chihuahuan rancher Ramon Lujan." Moreover, he noted that Schuster claimed he "bought the cattle from a San Simon rancher named Thompson," who he also accused of being a cattle thief who routinely sold beef to contractors.

23. Letter from Governor John C. Fremont to Secretary of Interior Carl Schurz, dated January 6, 1879. Cowboy Depredations File, U.S. Document [microfilm], Record Group 60, University of Arizona Library; Tucson, Arizona. About the allegation of a band of organized men in Arizona, Fremont commented: "This statement greatly surprises me.

Except for the occasional crime, relative to a border situation, no mention has come to me of any disturbances on the frontier. The authorities on our side have vigorously followed up every outrage, and Gen. Mariscal, the Governor of Sonora, has shown every disposition to cooperate effectively with us in maintaining good order and a friendly understanding."

24. Johnson, *John Ringo*, pp. 112-113.

25. Letter from Governor John C. Fremont to Secretary of Interior Carl Schurz, dated January 26, 1879. Cowboy Depredations File, U.S. Document [microfilm], Record Group 60, University of Arizona Library; Tucson, Arizona.

26. Cool, Paul, "Bob Martin: A Rustler in Paradise," p. 29, citing Juan N. Navarro to William M. Evarts, August 28, 1880.

27. Cool, Paul, "Bob Martin: A Rustler in Paradise," p. 31, citing Juan M. Zuloaga to Governor of Chihuahua, August 30, 1880.

28. *El Paso Times,* July 18, 1883.

29. Cool, Paul, "Bob Martin: A Rustler in Paradise," pp. 30-31.

30. *The Southwest,*(Silver City) August 10, 1880.

31. *The Southwest,*(Silver City) August 11, 1880.

32. There is no proof the Curly Bill Rogers and Curly Bill Brocius were the same man. Rogers' presence at San Simon nonetheless is an interesting coincidence to say the least. The *National Police Gazette,* on January 23, 1882, printed a picture of William A. Rogers, alias Curly Bill of Colorado, who was a marshal at St. Elmo, Colorado.

33. Reminiscences of J.C. Hancock. Arizona Historical Society Library, Tucson, Arizona.

34. The *Arizona Weekly Star,* on October 7, 1880, noted that four cowboys at San Simon took possession of a locomotive but could not use it because the fire was out in the boiler. About a month later, the *Arizona Weekly Star,* on November 4, 1880, alleged that Curly Bill was one of the four cowboys involved in the San Simon train incident.

35. *Arizona Weekly Star,* December 2, 1880; *Tucson Daily Citizen,* December 7, 1880; *Tucson Weekly Citizen,* December 11, 1880; *Arizona Daily Star,* December 9, 1880.

Chapter Four. THE MURDEROUS PISTOL

1. *Arizona Weekly Star,* November 4, 1880.

2. Statement of Wyatt Earp, *Tombstone Nugget*, November 17, 1881.

3. Copy of the appointment document in author's files courtesy Ben T. Traywick.

4. *Tombstone Daily Epitaph*, October 28, 1880.

5. *Tucson Daily Citizen*, December 27, 1880.

6. Ibid.

7. Ibid.

8. Ibid.

9. *Tombstone Daily Epitaph*, October 28, 1880; *Tucson Daily Citizen*, December 27, 1880.

10. *Tucson Daily Citizen*, December 27, 1880.

11. Ibid.

12. Ibid.

13. Ibid.

14. Ibid.

15. Ibid.

16. Ibid.

17. *Tombstone Daily Epitaph*, October 28, 1880.

18. *Tucson Daily Citizen*, December 27, 1880.

19. *Tombstone Daily Epitaph*, October 28, 1880.

20. Minutes of the Tombstone Common Council, Special Collections department, University of Arizona Library, Tucson.

21. *Arizona Weekly Star*, November 4, 1880.

22. *Tombstone Daily Epitaph*, October 29, 1880.

23. Record of Commitments, Pima County Records, Arizona Historil Society Library, Tucson.

24. Ibid.

25. *Tombstone Daily Epitaph*, November 1, 1880.

26. Cause 300, State of Texas vs. Robert Martin and William Bresnaham. El Paso County District Court Clerk's Office, El Paso, Texas.

27. Bailey, Lynn R., ed., *A Tenderfoot in Tombstone: The Private Journal of George Whitwell Parsons - The Turbulent Years, 1880 - 1882* (Tucson: Westernlore Press 1996), p. 183. Following an encounter with Curly Bill at the McLaury ranch on October 6, 1881, Parsons noted in his diary: "At McL's, was Arizona's most famous outlaw at the present time, Curly Bill."

Chapter Five. TERRITORY OF ARIZONA VS. WILLIAM BROCIUS

1. Following their arrest in El Paso Del Norte on May 22, 1878, Curly Bill and Bob Martin were in custody over five months until they escaped on November 2, 1878.

2. Record of Commitments, Pima County Records, Arizona Historil Society Library, Tucson.

3. *Arizona Daily Star*, December 22, 1880.

4. *Arizona Weekly Star*, December 2, 1880; *Tucson Daily Citizen*, December 7, 1880; *Tucson Weekly Citizen*, December 11, 1880; *Arizona Daily Star*, December 9, 1880.

5. Gatto, Steve, *Johnny Ringo* (Lansing: Protar House, 2002), pp. 37-38, 42. In May 1876, a group of men organized by Joe Olney, a/k/a Joe Hill, busted John Ringo and Scott Cooley from the Lampasas County jail. In June 1876, Burnet County, Texas, charged John Ringo with "aiding a prisoner to escape from the custody of a lawful officer."

6. *Arizona Daily Star*, on December 9, 1880.

7. *Arizona Daily Star*, December 22, 1880.

8. Ibid.

9. Ibid.

10. Ibid.

11. Ibid.

12. *Arizona Daily Star*, December 23, 1880.

13. *Arizona Daily Star*, December 25, 1880.

14. *Tucson Daily Citizen*, December 27, 1880.

15. *Silver City Enterpise*, September 5, 1884.

16. Breakenridge, William, *Helldorado: Bringing the Law to the Mesquite*, p. 132.

17. *Tombstone Nugget*, October 19, 1880. Record of Pima County Board of Supervisors 1880, Arizona Historical Society Library, Tucson, Arizona.

18. Gatto, Steve, *Johnny Ringo* (Lansing: Protar House, 2002), pp. 69-70. Record of Pima County Board of Supervisors 1880, Arizona Historical Society Library, Tucson, Arizona.

19. Anderson, "Posses and Politics in Pima County," *The Journal of Arizona History*, 1986, pp. 272-275.

20. Lake, Stuart, *Wyatt Earp, Frontier Marshal*, p. 245.

21. *Arizona Republic,* April 13, 1927. Article by J. C. Hancock entitled "Cattle Rustlers Take Charge of San Simon Poll." The story can also be found in Burns' *Tombstone,* p. 92. Yet, neither Hancock nor Burns mentions Wyatt Earp assisting Bob Paul obtain information in any way.

22. Record of Commitments, Pima County Records, Arizona Historical Society Library, Tucson. The Pima County Sheriff kept a daily log of the men confined in the county jail. Curly Bill provably was in the jail from October 28, 1880, until December 27, 1880.

Chapter Six. COME AND GET ME

1. Bailey, Lynn R., ed., *A Tenderfoot in Tombstone: The Private Journal of George Whitwell Parsons - The Turbulent Years, 1880 - 1882,* p. 118. On page 146, for his entry of May 13, 1881, Parsons further noted: "McKane the rough uncouth domine [clergymen] is a strange character . . . . He is the one 'Curly Bill' made dance and commanded to preach and pray, shot out lights, etc. at Charleston recently. He won't discuss the matter. He tells some strange stories for a minister."

2. *Arizona Daily Star,* January 27, 1881

3. *Arizona Daily Star,* January 27, 1881.

4. Ibid.

5. Ibid.

6. Ibid.

7. Ibid.

8. Ibid.

9. Ibid.

10. The Laws of Arizona (1881), Act 7, enacted by Eleventh Legislative Assembly of the Territory of Arizona, p. 4.

11. Judge Charles French's order that all district court cases that had originated in Cochise County must be transferred to that county was based on a sound legal basis. Included within the act creating Cochise County was Section 7, which provided for the cases originating in Cochise County to be transferred to the district court in that county.

12. Pima County Records, Arizona Historical Society Library, Tucson, Arizona.

13. *National Police Gazette*, February 1882.

14. *Tombstone Epitaph*, October 8, 1881. The *Epitaph* picked up the story from an article published in the *San Francisco Examiner* on October 3, 1881. The San Francisco article was forwarded to this author by Casey Tefertiller.

15. Ibid.

16. Ibid.

17. *Arizona Weekly Star*, February 17, 1881.

18. Letter from E. B. Pomroy, United States Attorney for Territory of Arizona, to Wayne MacVeagh, United States Attorney General, June 23, 1881. Cowboy Depredations File, U.S. Document [microfilm], Record Group 60, University of Arizona Library, Tucson, Arizona.

19. The *Tombstone Nugget*, on December 16, 1881, reported a rumor that Curly Bill, Billy Grounds, Zwing Hunt, Led Moore, and Jim Hughes had gathered together for the last time near Shakespeare. Therefore, it is reasonable to infer that these men were considered associates. Curly Bill, Billy Grounds, Zwing Hunt, and Led Moore were indicted for the same crime on December 2, 1881. Register of Actions, Cochise County Clerk's Office, Bisbee, Arizona.

20. Although it is impossible to be certain which men may have ridden with Curly Bill at various times, Bob Martin, Dick Lloyd, and Jim Wallace provably interacted with Brocius. Sandy King and Russian Bill are often connected to Curly Bill by old-timers. Milt and Will Hicks were likely associates of Curly Bill and in the case of Territory vs. Curly Bill-Hicks et al, Sheriff Behan sent a deputy to El Paso looking for them in February 1882.

21. Breakenridge, William, *Helldorado: Bringing the Law to the Mesquite*, p. 114.

22. Reminiscences of Melvin Jones. Arizona Historical Society Library, Tucson, Arizona.

23. Breakenridge, William, *Helldorado: Bringing the Law to the Mesquite*, pp. 114-115.

24. *Arizona Weekly Star*, March 10, 1881.

Chapter Seven. THE DEPUTY ASSESSOR

1. *Tombstone Epitaph*, April 6, 1881.

2. Breakenridge, William, *Helldorado: Bringing the Law to the*

Mesquite, p. 132.

3. Breakenridge, William, *Helldorado: Bringing the Law to the Mesquite*, p. 131.

4. The Laws of Arizona (1881), Act 7, enacted by Eleventh Legislative Assembly of the Territory of Arizona, p. 4.

5. Breakenridge, William, *Helldorado: Bringing the Law to the Mesquite*, p. 132.

6. Ibid.

7. Ibid.

8. Breakenridge, William, *Helldorado: Bringing the Law to the Mesquite*, p. 132.

9. *Silver City Enterprise*, October 17, 1884. The account reportedly came from Dave Wood, who was at the time a candidate for sheriff in Dona Ana County, New Mexico.

10. The *Silver City Enterprise*, on November 23, 1883, published a similar but earlier verison of the "Curly Bill coin-pistol trick."

Chapter Eight. THE NOTED DESPERADO SHOT

1. Breakenridge, William, *Helldorado: Bringing the Law to the Mesquite*, p. 165.

2. Ibid.

3. Ibid.

4. Breakenridge, William, *Helldorado: Bringing the Law to the Mesquite*, p. 166.

5. Ibid.

6. Breakenridge, William, *Helldorado: Bringing the Law to the Mesquite*, p. 167.

7. Ibid.

8. Reminiscences of J.C. Hancock. Arizona Historical Society Library, Tucson, Arizona.

9. Reminiscences of Robert Boller. Arizona Historical Society Library, Tucson, Arizona.

10. Reminiscences of Melvin Jones. Arizona Historical Society Library, Tucson, Arizona.

11. Marks. Paula Mitchell, *And Die in The West*, p. 167. The *Arizona Weekly Star*, on July 8, 1881, printed Harper's letter:

Thomas Harper's Letter

The following letter written by Thomas Harper, who was executed at Tucson the 9th inst, will apply to many besides Curley Bill, to whom it was addressed. Until this circumstance of the killing of Talleday, Harper bore the reputation of being a quiet and peaceable man, although his associates and surroundings were bad:

Tucson, July 7, 1881

Friend Curley: By the time you recieve this, I will in all likelihood be past seeing or writing to you, as you well know I am under sentence of death. I am to be hanged tomorrow, but at what hour I do not as yet know. Some unknown persons in town have interested themselves in my behalf and petitioned the Governor, but as yet there has been no answer from him. I have made up my mind for the worst and I think I willl face death like a man; I must go some time, so now, when I have found all chances of a reprieve of commutation of sentence lost, I am prepared to meet it in its worst form.

Curley, you are aware that I am not in the habit of lecturing any man, but in this case you may remember the words, of a dying man, (for I am to all intended purposes such), and perhaps give heed to them. When I killed that man I believed that I was acting in self defense. I thought my life was in danger from him; and acting under the influence of that feeling, I shot. A jury has found me guilty of murder, a Judge has sentenced me, and by this time to morrow, (2 o'clock) I shall have ceased to exist. Curley, I want you to take warning by me. Do not be too handy with a pistol. Keep cool, and never fire at a man except in the actual defense of your life. You must stand a heap from a man before you kill him. Words do not hurt, so you must never mind what is said to aggravate you. As I said before, don't try and hurt a man until he actually assaults and hurts you; but above all things never hunt a man.

Give my kind regards to any of my old friends whom you may chance to meet, and tell them to take warning by me. I bear no man ill and I think I am going to die in peace. Hoping you will take heed of what I write, I am as ever, your unfortunate friend.

Thomas Harper

To Wm. H. Brocius, care G. W. Turner, San Simon.

12. Ibid.

13. Lake, Stuart, *Wyatt Earp, Frontier Marshal,* p. 272.

14. The *Arizona Weekly Star,* on June 23, 1881, commented: "The killing of Bill Leonard and 'Harry the Kid' at Eureka, N.M. by the Haslett brothers, a full account of which appeared in the STAR of Sunday morning, has been summarily avenged. It appears that a cowboy named Crane organized and got a band of congenial spirits in the work of vengeance. They followed the Haslett boys for some twenty-five miles from Eureka before they overtook them, and as soon as they came up with them the fight to the death commenced. The Haslett boys were game and made a brave fight killing two and wounding three of the Crane party but being overpowered were finally killed." However, the *Tombstone Nugget,* the day earlier carried a slighly different story of the incident: "The boys [Hasletts] were playing cards for pastime in West McFadden's saloon, when about fifteen or twenty men came down on them by surprise, and they did not have a chance to protect themselves."

15. John Ringo was in Austin, Texas, on May 2, 1881, where he was arrested by Ben Thompson. *Austin Daily Statesman,* May 3, 1881. Exactly when Ringo left Arizona is not known, but considering that he was in Texas during earlier May, it is reasonable to conclude that he left sometime around mid-April 1881.

Chapter Nine. FRONTERAS MASSACRE

1. *Tombstone Nugget,* June 9, 1881.

2. Ibid.

3. *Tombstone Daily Epitaph*, September 10, 1881.

4. Ibid.

5. Ibid.

6. *Arizona Weekly Star*, June 23, 1881.

7. Reminiscences of James C. Hancock. Arizona Historical Society Library, Tucson, Arizona. It should be remembered that Hancock was not present during the incident and his recollections were made years later based on what he claimed he had heard.

8. Ibid.

9. Walter Noble Burns was one of the first to mistake the attack near Fronteras, Mexico, as occuring in Skeleton Canyon. Burns, *Tombstone*, pp. 95-106. Since then many writers, including this author, have repeated the error. See, e.g., Marks, Paula Mitchell Marks, *And Die in the West* (New York: William Morrow, 1989), p. 170; Erwin, Richard, *The Truth About Wyatt Earp* (Carpinteria: The OK Corral Press, 1993), pp. 196-200; and Tefertiller, Casey, *Wyatt Earp, The Life Behind the Legend* (New York" John Wiley and Sons, Inc., 1997), p. 92. Nonetheless, Skeleton Canyon, which is in the United States, is fifty miles from the Mexican town of Fronteras.

10. *San Francisco Evening Bulletin*, August 13, 1881.

11. *Tombstone Nugget*, August 16, 1881; *Arizona Weekly Star*, August 25, 1881. In recent years some authors have speculated that the Earp brothers and Doc Holliday carried out the Guadalupe Canyon massacre. The historical record shows that scenario is without merit.

12. Gatto, *Real Wyatt Earp*, pp. 92-93., citing Traywick, Ben T., *The Clantons of Tombstone* (Tombstone: Red Marie's Books 1996), p.77.

13. *Arizona Weekly Citizen*, September 4, 1881.

14. Cowboy Depredations File, U.S. Document [microfilm], Record Group 60, University of Arizona Library, Tucson, Arizona.

15. Cowboy Depredations File, U.S. Document [microfilm], Record Group 60, University of Arizona Library, Tucson, Arizona. See also Tefertiller, *Wyatt Earp*, pp. 252-253.

16. Breakenridge, *Helldorado*, p. 110.

17. Breakenridge, *Helldorado*, p. 142.

18. Ibid.

19. *Tombstone Epitaph*, October 5, 6, 1881.

20. Bailey, Lynn R., ed., *A Tenderfoot in Tombstone: The Private*

Journal of George Whitwell Parsons - The Turbulent Years, 1880 - 1882, p. 182.

21. Lake, Stuart N., *Wyatt Earp, Frontier Marshal* (New York: Houghton Mifflin, 1931), p. 273.

22. Indictment of William Brocius, George Chambers Collection, Arizona Historical Society Library, Tucson.

23. Ibid.

24. Criminal Register of Actions, Cochise County Court Clerk's Office, Bisbee, Arizona: Territory of Arizona vs. William Brocius, Larceny Indictment, December 2, 1881.

25. Indictment of William Brocius, George Chambers Collection, Arizona Historical Society Library, Tucson.

26. Criminal Register of Actions, Cochise County Court Clerk's Office, Bisbee, Arizona. See appendix of this book for facsimiles.

27. *Tombstone Epitaph*, December 8, 1881.

28. *Tombstone Nugget,* December 16, 1881.

Chapter Ten. EARP BOYS VS. COWBOYS

1. *Tombstone Epitaph*, October 27, 1881.

2. Testimony of Ike Clanton published by the *Tombstone Nugget* on October 29, 1881, and November 3, 1881.

3. Gatto, Steve, *Real Wyatt Earp* (Silver City: High-Lonesome Press, 2000), p. 107, note 20.

4. *Tombstone Nugget*, October 30, 1881.

5. *Tombstone Nugget*, October 30, 1881; Gatto, Steve, *Real Wyatt Earp* (Silver City: High-Lonesome Press, 2000), pp. 110-124.

6. Ibid.

7. Ibid.

8. *Tombstone Epitaph*, December 1, 1881.

9. Cowboy Depredations File, U.S. Document [microfilm], Record Group 60, University of Arizona Library; Tucson, Arizona.

10. Statement of Wyatt Earp, *Tombstone Nugget,* November 17, 1881.

11. *Tombstone Epitaph,* on December 29, 1881, the morning after Virgil Earp was shot, made a reference to the rumored threats.

12. *Tombstone Nugget*, December 16, 1881; *Tombstone Epitaph,* December 18, 1881.

13. *Tombstone Epitaph*, December 18, 1881.
14. *Tombstone Epitaph*, January 13, 1882.
15. *Tombstone Epitaph*, December 15, 1881.
16. Ibid.
17. *Tombstone Nugget*, December 15, 1881; December 16, 1881.
18. Lake, *Frontier Marshal*, p. 333.
19. *Tombstone Epitaph*, December 29, 1881.
20. Bailey, Lynn R., ed., *A Tenderfoot in Tombstone: The Private Journal of George Whitwell Parsons - The Turbulent Years, 1880 - 1882* (Tucson: Westernlore Press 1996), pp. 198-199.
21. Curly Bill was neither implicated in the crime at the time by the local newspapers that reported the incident nor later charged with the crime, as the Clanton brothers were in late January 1882.
22. *Tombstone Epitaph*, December 30, 1881. Mrs. Colyer made no reference to Curly Bill being a leader of the cowboy gang.
23. *Tombstone Daily Epitaph*, January 10, 1882; Marks, *And Die in the West*, pp. 324-325; Tefertiller, *Wyatt Earp*, pp. 179-181.
24. Ibid.
25. *Los Angeles Times*, January 26, 1882; *San Francisco Evening Bulletin*, January 26, 1882; *San Diego Union*, January 26, 1882.
26. *Tombstone Nugget*, January 31, 1882.
27. Lake, *Frontier Marshal*, p. 314.
28. In an article attributed to Wyatt Earp and published by the *San Francisco Examiner* on August 9, 1896, Curly Bill is accused of participating in the stagecoach robbery of January 6, 1882, showing that Lake was not the person who originated the claim.
29. *Tombstone Nugget*, March 14, 1882.
30. Lake, *Frontier Marshal*, p. 314.
31. Ibid.
32. *Tombstone Nugget*, on March 18, 1882.
33. *Tombstone Epitaph*, January 24, 1882.
34. Lake, *Frontier Marshal*, p. 315.
35. *Tombstone Epitaph*, January 24, 1882.
36. *Tombstone Nugget*, January 31, 1882.
37. Ibid.
38. The *Tombstone Epitaph* of February 3, 1881, published the proceedings of the Clanton trial for the shooting of Virgil Earp.
39. *Tombstone Nugget*, January 31, 1882.

40. Ibid.

41. Ibid.

42. *Tombstone Epitaph*, March 22, 1882; *Tombstone Epitaph*, March 22, 1882.

43. *Tombstone Epitaph*, December 30, 1881.

44. Lake, *Frontier Marshal*, p. 335.

45. Letter from Wyatt Earp to Walter Noble Burns, March 15, 1927. Walter Noble Burns Collection, University of Arizona Library, Special Collections, Tucson, Arizona.

46. *Arizona Daily Star*, March 22, 1882.

47. Ibid.

48. Ibid.

49. *Tombstone Epitaph*, March 23, 1882.

50. Ibid.

51. Cochise County Records, MS 180, Box 8, folder 83; Sheriff John Behan's financial reports, January-April 1882. Arizona Historical Society Library, Tucson, Arizona.

52. *Tombstone Nugget*, December 16, 1881.

Chapter Eleven. BATTLE AT BURLEIGH SPRINGS

1. *Tombstone Nugget*, March 26, 1882.

2. Ibid.

3. *Tombstone Epitaph*, March 23, 1882.

4. Ibid.

5. Ibid.

6. Ibid.

7. *Tombstone Nugget*, March 26, 1882.

8. Carmony, Neil B., ed., *Next Stop: Tombstone - George Hand's Contention City Diary 1882,* (Tucson: Trial to Yesterday Books), 1995, p. 12.

9. Bailey, *Parsons Journal*, pp. 214-215.

10. Cochise County Records, MS 180, Box 8, folder 83; Sheriff John Behan's financial reports, January-April 1882. Arizona Historical Society Library, Tucson, Arizona. On February 17, 1882, Sheriff Behan expensed $56.20 for a deputy's mileage to El Paso in search of the defendants in the case: "Territory vs. Curly Bill-Hicks et al."

11. The *Tombstone Nugget's* article of March 25, 1882, alleged

that two posses, totalling nearly forty men, were after the Earps. However, the author has concluded that the report of a second posse, organized at Charleston, was inaccurate. Sheriff Behan's financial reports housed at the Arizona Historical Society (Cochise County Records, MS 180, box 8, folder 83) list the men who joined Behan's posse on March 22, 1882. Eighteen men served for ten days, a few others from one to five days.

12. Cochise County Records, MS 180, Box 8, folder 83; Sheriff John Behan's financial reports, January-April 1882. Arizona Historical Society Library, Tucson, Arizona. These papers list the men who joined Behan's posse on March 22, 1882, the number of days each served, and how much each man was paid (at a rate of $5 per day). Curly Bill Brocius was not among the posse men who helped Sheriff Behan chase the Earp party.

13. Diarist George Hand, a Tucson saloon keeper, was visiting Contention City and wrote the following remarks in his journal: "Friday [March] 24. The cow boys [Behan's posse], twenty or more, have been prowling around all morning. They are well mounted, well armed and seem intent on biz. They are in search of the Earp party who took breakfast 2 miles above here this morning. 3 P.M.—they [the posse] again came from the direction of Tombstone, watered their horses here and started again at the double quick for Kinnear's ranch." The following day, March 25, 1882, Hand noted: "Sheriff Behan and posse arrived here this evening. Raining so hard they put their horses in stable." Carmony, Neil B., ed., *Next Stop: Tombstone - George Hand's Contention City Diary 1882*, (Tucson: Trial to Yesterday Books), 1995, pp. 9-11.

14. *Arizona Daily Star*, March 26, 1882.

15. Ibid.

16. Bailey, Lynn R., ed., *A Tenderfoot in Tombstone: The Private Journal of George Whitwell Parsons - The Turbulent Years, 1880 - 1882*, pp. 214-215.

17. *Arizona Daily Star*, March 26, 1882.

18. Ibid.

19. Ibid.

20. In *Wyatt Earp, Frontier Marshal* (New York: Houghton Mifflin, 1931), p. 338, Stuart Lake identified the site of Wyatt's purported fight with Curly Bill as "Iron Springs." However, on later maps the

designation is Mescal Springs. Mescal Springs is located about twenty miles west of Tombstone. The U.S. Forest Service map of the area places the spring in section 32, township 19 south, range 19 east. John Flood's manuscript written ca. 1926, also places the encounter at Iron Springs. So does a letter written by Wyatt Earp to Walter Noble Burns on March 15, 1927.

21. *Tombstone Nugget,* March 26, 1882; Carmony, Neil B., ed., *Next Stop: Tombstone - George Hand's Contention City Diary 1882,* (Tucson: Trial to Yesterday Books), 1995, pp. 9-12.

22. In *Wyatt Earp, Frontier Marshal* (New York: Houghton Mifflin, 1931), pp. 347-348, Stuart Lake changed Wright and Kraker's account in order to substantiate Wyatt's claim to have killed Curly Bill. According to Lake's version, Wright and Kraker witnessed Frank Patterson drive a wagon up the trail to the spring, where a "lifeless body was lifted into it." Lake's tale has Wright and Kraker observing that two men were wounded—"Milt Hicks in the arm and Johnny Barnes in the upper chest or shoulder." Lake then declared that Wright and Kraker "recognized the dead man as Curly Bill." In addition, "they saw a Wells-Fargo gun and a pair of ivory-handled, gold-trimmed Colt's put in the wagon beside the body." Lake then wrote the Wright and Kraker told Wells-Fargo detective John Thacker where to find the body and Thacker went to verify Curly Bill's death. Of course, Lake's version is complete nonsense—Wright and Kraker told their account to both Tombstone newspapers, and they made no such claims at the time.

23. A thousand dollars was a considerable amount of money in 1882. If anyone had proof of Curly Bill's death or personal knowledge of the secret location of Curly Bill's grave, the reward seemingly would have provided great incentive to reveal the information.

24. Tefertiller, *Wyatt Earp*, p. 240.

25. Curly Bill "ephemera" file and the James C. Hancock file and clippings book, Arizona Historical Society Library, Tucson, Arizona; *Arizona Republic*, October 14, 1951, "Curly Bill Story Has 4 endings" by Grace MCool.

26. *Tombstone Nugget,* December 16, 1882; *Arizona Daily Star,* March 26, 1882; *Tombstone Nugget,* February 21, 1882.

27. There are no newspaper reports, court documents, or diary entries from December 16, 1881, to March 25, 1882, (the day after the shootout at Mescal Springs) that place Curly Bill in Arizona.

28. The news of Curly Bill's death traveled to major cities, like San Francisco and Chicago, and smaller cities in the region. However, a search of several newspapers throughout the Southwest has conviced the author that many smaller communities did not print the story in the local newspapers.

29. Breakenridge, William, *Helldorado: Bringing the Law to the Mesquite,* pp. 177-178.

30. *Silver City Enterprise,* March 26, 1886.

31. *National Police Gazette,* January 23, 1882.

32. *The Southwest,*(Silver City) August 10, 1880; *The Southwest,*(Silver City) August 11, 1880.

33. Reminiscences of Melvin Jones. Arizona Historical Society Library, Tucson, Arizona.

34. Reminiscences of Melvin Jones. Arizona Historical Society Library, Tucson, Arizona.

35. Reminiscences of J.C. Hancock. Arizona Historical Society Library, Tucson, Arizona.

36. *The New Southwest and Grant County Herald,*(Silver City) April 15, 1882.

37. Ibid.

38. Rasch, Phil, "The Resurrection of Pony Deal." Phil Rasch Collection, MS 677, Box 1, File 1, Arizona Historical Society, Tucson, Arizona. According to Rasch, Deal was "extradited from Chihuahua by Governor Lionel Sheldon and turned over to Sheriff Guadalupe Ascarte, of Dona Ana County." (Office of the Secretary of the Interior, Patents and Miscellaneous Division, Proceedings of the Executive Office of the Territory of New Mexico, 1875-1896). Deal was tried in New Mexcio on three counts of "buying stolen cattle and larceny of cattle." After being found guilty, he was sentenced "to five years in the territorial penitentiary." Three years later, on March 14, 1887, Deal received a pardon and disappeared into obscurity.

39. Erwin, Allen A., *The Southwest of John H. Slaughter, 1841-1922,* Second Printing (Spokane: The Aurthur H. Clark Company, 1997).

40. *El Paso Times,* June 26, 1883.

41. *Arizona Weekly Citizen,* July 14, 1883.

42. *Arizona Republic,* October 14, 1951, "Curly Bill Story Has 4 Endings" by Grace McCool.

43. Ibid.

44. Reminiscences of J.C. Hancock. Arizona Historical Society Library, Tucson, Arizona.

45. Miller, Nyle, and Snell, Joseph, *Great Gunfighters of the Kansas Cowtowns, 1867-1886* (Lincoln: Bison Books, 1967), pp. 361-366.

46. *Field and Farm*, August 17, 1893.

47. Ibid.

48. A series of three articles attributed to Wyatt Earp were published on consecutive Sundays by the *San Francisco Examiner*, August 2, 9, 16, 1896; Earp, Wyatt, ed., Carmony, Neil, "How I Routed a Gang of Arizona Outlaws and Other Stories" (Tucson: Trail To Yesterday Books, 1995).

49. *San Francisco Examiner*, August 2, 1896; Earp, Wyatt, ed., Carmony, Neil, "How I Routed a Gang of Arizona Outlaws and Other Stories" (Tucson: Trail To Yesterday Books, 1995), p. 14.

50. Ibid.

51. *San Francisco Examiner*, August 9, 1896; Earp, Wyatt, ed., Carmony, Neil, "How I Routed a Gang of Arizona Outlaws and Other Stories" (Tucson: Trail To Yesterday Books, 1995), p. 18.

52. Ibid., p. 22.

53. Arrest warrants in the case were issued for Pony Deal, Al Tiebot, and Charles Haws. Curly Bill was not implicated in the crime at the time and no warrant was issued for his arrest in the matter.

54. Lake, Stuart N., *Wyatt Earp, Frontier Marshal* (New York: Houghton Mifflin, 1931), p. 340. John Flood's manuscript contains another story about Curly Bill using the stolen Wells, Fargo shotgun at Mescal Springs. As if the stolen shotgun story wasn't bad enough, Lake also claimed that Wyatt "saw the ivory butts of Jim Hume's pet six-guns in Hume's fancy holsters at Curly Bill's waist as clearly as could be." Hume's pistols had been stolen during a second robbery in January. Nevertheless, Curly Bill was not implicated in that crime either and was not believed to have taken Hume's pistols. Instead, Alex Arnold was the suspected robber who was believed to be in possession of Hume's prized weapons. The *Tombstone Nugget*, on March 18, 1882, made the following comments about the pistols: "Alex Arnold, you are wanted! It is said you helped to rob the Benson and Tombstone stage on the 8th of January. That would not have made so much

difference, but you were impertinent enough to deprive the valiant and garrulous Hume, high muck-a-muck detective for Wells, Fargo & Co., of his two Smith & Wesson pistols. This was very naughty on your part, and he has been abusing the people of this section ever since. He says you are about 5 feet 8 or 10 inches high, weigh about 150, and have a small mustache, small eyes, deep set, and are about 33 years of age. You will observe, Aleck [sic], that he was cool enough to note this, but all the same, you have those two pistols, and as he is getting old and peevish, you had better send them back, so the boys will quit joshing him."

55. Breakenridge, William, *Helldorado: Bringing the Law to the Mesquite,* p. 176. William Lutley was the Tombstone man who informed Breakenridge that Alex Arnold and Pink Truly told him the details of the battle at the spring. Breakenridge / Helldorado File, Houghton Mifflin Collection, Houghton Library, Harvard University, Cambridge, Massachusetts. Courtesy of Neil Carmony.

56. *Tombstone Nugget,* April 1, 1882.

57. Ibid.

58. *Arizona Weekly Star,* April 6, 1882.

59. Ibid.

60. Ibid.

61. Ibid.

62. Lake, Carolyn, ed., *Undercover for Wells Fargo: The Unvarnished Recollections of Fred Dodge* (Boston: Houghton Mifflin, 1969), pp. 233-235, 242-243. Despite Dodge's unsupported assertion that Barnes told him that Curly Bill was killed in the shootout at the spring, John Barnes was not at the spring when the fight happened. In actuality, Sheriff John Behan's financial records indicate that Barnes was riding with his posse that day and rode to Kinnear's ranch the day of the fight. Barnes was later paid $50 for ten days of posse work from March 22, 1882, to March 31, 1882. Cochise County Records, MS 180, Box 8, folder 83; Sheriff John Behan's financial reports, January-April 1882. Arizona Historical Society Library, Tucson, Arizona.

62. Many of Fred Dodge's statements made decades later cannot be confirmed, and many people have questioned the veracity of his claims. He asserted that he came to Tombstone as an undercover man for Wells, Fargo. According to Dodge, the only man who knew of his undercover position was Wells, Fargo president, John J. Valentine—the

man who hired him. No Wells, Fargo employment records for Fred Dodge for the years he was in Tombstone have ever been found.

Some writers and historians have seriously questioned Fred Dodge as a trustworthy source. According to Don Chaput, Virgil Earp's biographer, Dodge's claim to have been an undercover agent for Wells, Fargo in Tombstone had no basis in fact. "After years of investigating . . . I have concluded that Fred Dodge was no more undercover [for Wells, Fargo in Tombstone] than Jesse James was a clergyman . . . ." Chaput, Don, *Buckskin Frank Leslie* (Tucson: Westernlore Press, 2000). The author of this book agrees with Chaput's assessment. Robert Chandler, historian and senior researcher for Wells Fargo Bank, made the following statement after reveiwing Fred Dodge's claim that he was a secret agent for Wells, Fargo: "I do not believe it." Chandler concluded, "In my opinion, Fred Dodge idolized the older Wyatt Earp. When Stuart Lake brought them together in 1928, Dodge—the former faro dealer—romanticized his disreputable arrival in Tombstone. Claiming to have been a Wells, Fargo detective was a ploy that placed him in the forefront of the action and made him a peer of the great Wyatt." Chandler, Robert J. "Under Cover for Wells Fargo: A Review Essay." *Journal of Arizona History.* Volume 41, Number 1, Spring 2000, pp. 83-96.

63. Another example of Wyatt's penchant for making false claims is his tale of killing John Ringo on his way out of Arizona. In an article about John Ringo's death published in *Wild West Magazine*, February 2000, Casey Tefertiller acknowledged that it was impossible for Wyatt Earp to have killed John Ringo on his way out of Arizona. However, he maintained that "Earp did not make the claim to his biographer Stuart Lake, nor did he make it in an interview with writer Walter Noble Burns." Rather than consider that Wyatt Earp may have fabricated the claim, Tefertiller concluded that "Earp neither killed Ringo nor ever actually made the claim that he did so." Nonetheless, there are four independent and separate sources (Forrestine Hooker—1919, John Flood—1926, Frank Lockwood—1926, and Frederick Bechdolt—1927) corroborating the claim that Earp said he killed Ringo while leaving Arizona. Bechdolt wrote in a letter to William Breakenridge that Earp told him that "he (Earp) and several others, including Doc Holliday, were riding out on one of a number of expeditions from the Hooker ranch, looking for Ringo and Curly Bill when they encountered Ringo"—who Earp killed.

Of course, Earp's story is provably false because Ringo died four months after the gunfight at the spring where Wyatt claimed Curly Bill was killed. Thus, the most reasonable conclusion is that Wyatt Earp did, indeed, make the bogus claim that he killed John Ringo. Bechdolt letter Courtesy of Neil Carmony. Breakenridge / Helldorado File, Houghton Mifflin Collection, Houghton Library, Harvard University, Cambridge, Massachusetts.

    64. *Tombstone Epitaph*, March 27, 1882.

    65. The author prefers to use the term "Battle at Burleigh Springs" because the *Tombstone Epitaph*'s intentional misrepresentation of the location of the fight set the tone for the incident and resulting aftermath of rumor and gossip. In the author's opinion, Curly Bill was not present at the spring or killed on that day, nor was anyone else killed—the lone death from the famous "Battle at Burleigh Springs" was a horse.

BIBLIOGRAPHY

BOOKS

Alexander, Bob. *John H. Behan, Sacrificed Sheriff.* Silver City: High-Lonesome Press, 2002.

Artrip, Louise and Fullen, *Memoirs of Daniel Fore (Jim) Chisholm and the Chisholm Trail,* (Booneville: Artrip Publications, 1949).

_____. *Memoirs of Late Daniel Fore (Jim) Chisholm and the Chisholm Trail.* Booneville: Artrip Publications, 1959.

Bailey, Lynn R., ed. *A Tenderfoot in Tombstone: The Private Journal of George Whitwell Parsons - The Turbulent Year, 1880-1882.* Tucson: Westernlore Press, 1996.

_____. *Tombstone From a Woman's Point of View: The Correspondence of Clara Spalding Brown, July 7, 1880, to November 14, 1882.* Tucson: Westernlore Press, 1998.

Bakarich, Sara Grace. *Gunsmoke, The True Story of Old Tombstone.* Tombstone: Tombstone Press, 1954.

Ball, Larry, D. *The United States Marshals of New Mexico and Arizona territories, 1846-1912.* Albuquerque: University of New Mexico Press, 1978.

Bechdolt, Frederick. *When the West Was Young.* New York: The Century Company, 1922.

Breakenridge, William M. *Helldorado, Bringing the Law to the Mesquite.* New York: Houghton Mifflin, 1928.

Brosius, Lewis Walton. *Geneaology of Henry and Mary Brosius and their Descendents* (Wilmington: Self Published, 1928).

Burns, Walter Noble, *Tombstone, An Iliad of the Southwest* (New York: Doubleday, 1927)

Burrows, Jack. *John Ringo, The Gunfighter Who Never Was.* Tucson: University of Arizona Press, 1987.

Chaput, Don. *"Buckskin" Frank Leslie.* Tucson: Westernlore Press, 1999.

Erwin, Richard, *The Truth About Wyatt Earp.* Carpinteria: The OK Corral Press, 1993.

Flood, John Henry Jr. *Wyatt Earp.* Riverside: Earl Chafin, 1997.

Gatto, Steve. *John Ringo: The Reputation of a Deadly Gunman.* Tucson: San Simon Publishing, 1995.

_____. *Wyatt Earp: A Biography of a Western Lawman.* Tucson: San Simon Publishing, 1997.

_____. *Real Wyatt Earp.* Silver City: High-Lonesome Press, 2000.

_____. *Johnny-Behind-the-Deuce: An account of the killing of Philip Schneider, Charleston, A.T, January 14, 1881.* Tucson: San Simon Publishing, 1998.

_____. *Alias Curly Bill: The Life and Times of William Brocius.* Tucson: Privately printed. 2000.

_____. *Johnny Ringo.* Lansing: Protar House. 2002.

Gillett, James B. *Six Years With The Texas Rangers.* Austin: Von Boeckmann-Jones Company, 1921.

Hooker, Forrestine Cooper. *An Arizona Vendetta: The Truth about Wyatt Earp* circa 1919-1920. Riverside: Earl Chafin Press, 1998.

Johnson, David. *John Ringo.* Stillwater: Barbed Wire Press, 1996.

Lake, Carolyn, ed. *Undercover for Wells Fargo: The Unvarnished Recollections of Fred Dodge.* Boston: Houghton Mifflin, 1969.

Lake, Stuart N. *Wyatt Earp: Frontier Marshal.* New York: Houghton Mifflin, 1931.

Lockwood, Frank C. *Pioneer Days in Arizona.* New York: The MacMillan Company, 1932.

Marks, Paula Mitchell. *And Die in the West.* New York: William Morrow, 1989.

Miller, Nyle H., and Joseph W. Snell. *Great Gunfighters of the Kansas Cowtowns, 1867-1886.* Lincoln: University of Nebraska Press, 1967.

Nolan, Frederick. *The Lincoln County War: A Documentary History.* Norman: University of Oklahoma Press, 1992.

Sonnichsen, C. L. *I'll Die Before I'll Run.* New York: Harper & Company, 1951.

_____. *Ten Texas Feuds.* Albuquerque: University of New Mexico Press, 1957.

_____. *El Paso Salt War.* El Paso: Hetzog, 1961.

_____. *Pass of the North: Four Centuries on the Rio Grande.* El Paso: Texas Western Press, 1968.

Tefertiller, Casey. *Wyatt Earp, The Life Behind the Legend.* New York: John Wiley and Sons, Inc., 1997.

Timmons, W. H., *El Paso: A Borderlands History.* El Paso: Texas Western Press, 1990.

Traywick, Ben T. *John Peters Ringo: Mythical Gunfighter.* Tombstone: Red Marie's Books, 1987.

_____. *Clantons of Tombstone.* Tombstone: Red Marie's Books, 1996.

Magazines and Periodicals

Anderson, Mike. "Posses and Politics in Pima County: The administration of Sheriff Charlie Shibell." *Journal of Arizona History.* Volume 27, No. 3, Autumn 1986, pp. 253-282.

Brand, Peter. "The Escape of 'Curly Bill' Brocius." Western Outlaw Lawman Association *Quarterly,* 2000.

Chandler, Robert J. "Under Cover for Wells Fargo: A Review Essay." *Journal of Arizona History.* Volume 41, Number 1, Spring 2000, pp. 83 96.

Chaput, Don. "Fred Dodge: Undercover Agent or Con Man?" National Outlaw and Lawman Association *Quarterly,* Vol. XXV, No. 1 (January - March.), 2000, 10-15.

Cool, Paul. "Bob Martin: A Rustler in Paridise." Western Outlaw Lawman Association *Quarterly,* 2003.

Gatto, Steve. "Johnny Ringo, Land and Cattle Speculator." National Outlaw Lawman Association *Quarterly.* Vol.18, No. 4, 1994, pp. 9-10.

Hill, Janaloo. "Yours Until Death, William Grounds." *True West,* April 1973, pp. 14-15, 54-59.

Johnson, David. "Daniel Hoerster and the 'Mason County War.'" National Outlaw and Lawman Association *Quarterly*, Vol. IX. No. 3 (Winter), 1985, pp. 15-18.

_____. "G. W. Gladden - Hard Luck Warrior." National Outlaw and Lawman Association *Quarterly*, Vol. XV. No. 3 (July - Sept.), 1991, pp.1, 3-6.

_____. "A Feudist By Any Other Name." National Outlaw and Lawman Association *Quarterly*, Vol. XVIII. No. 3 (July -Sept.), 1994, pp. 13-18.

Nolan, Fred. "Boss Rustler: The Life and Crimes of John Kinney, Part 1." *True West.* Vol. 43, No. 9, September 1996.

Rasch, Phil. "The Resurrection of Pony Diehl." Los Angeles Westerners *Branding Iron.* December 1957.

NEWSPAPERS

Arizona

Arizona Republic
Prescott *Arizona Gazette*
Clifton Clarion
Copper Era
Douglas Daily Dispatch
Phoenix Gazette
Tombstone Daily Epitaph
Tombstone *Daily Nugget*
Tombstone *Weekly Epitaph*
Tombstone *Weekly Nugget*
Tucson *Arizona Citizen*
Tucson *Arizona Daily Star*
Tucson *Arizona Weekly Citizen*
Tucson *Arizona Weekly Star*

California
Los Angeles Times
San Diego Union
San Francisco Evening Bulletin
San Franciso Examiner

Colorado
Field and Farm
Denver Republican
Denver Tribune
Pueblo Chiefton

Kansas
Ford County Globe
Dodge City Times

Missouri
Liberty Tribune

New Mexico
Mesilla Valley Independent
Grant County Herald
Silver City Enterprise
Thirty-Four
The Southwest

Texas
Austin Statesman
Austin Weekly Statesman
Dallas Herald
El Paso Times

Index

About The Author

Steve Gatto has been researching for the past fifteen years early Tombstone and the rowdy frontiersmen who made the boom town famous. Steve divides his time between Lansing, Michigan, where he practices law, and Tucson, Arizona, where he continues to study the history of Cochise County. He is the author of *The Real Wyatt Earp* (2000) and *Johnny Ringo* (2002).